Korean Essential Vocabulary 6000

Any foreigner who studies Korean must inevitably know,
**6,000 vocabulary selected by
The National Academy of the Korean Language**
The classification with notation A,B,C by the order of frequency

compiled by **Lee Jae-wook**

한글파크

Introduction
Foreword

While English and Chinese have been influencing over the world as world's languages, Korean has been staying at the level as a regional language all the time. But, recently, based on the Korean currents of many countries through the world beginning with southeastern Asian countries, the enthusiasm to learn Korean is keep increasing.

In case of China, Korean has become the second foreign language defeating Japanese and Korean language departments of universities in China have become so popular that the students of Korean language departments of universities in China are secured of jobs when they become sophomores.

It is definitely encouraging that more and more Japanese are learning Korean influenced by Korean dramas. Now, Korean is hardening it's position as a major foreign language throughout the area of southeastern Asia.

Introduction
Foreword

In accordance with such atmosphere, universities in Korea are exerting their full efforts to internationalize Korean by various ways such as opening Korean language teaching centers in southeastern Asia.

But, despite such current status, there has not been a good teaching material worthy of mention furnished by Korean. Recent phenomena that more than 300 Korean language study books have been poured out and Korean language teaching centers have been established in Korea too are composing beneficial conditions to accelerate the distribution of Korean.

The writer has been trying to develop a Korean language study book suitable to foreigners while teaching Korean in universities and private schools for more than 10years' residence in China. It goes without saying that the fastest way to learn a foreign language well is obtaining a good perception of it's grammatical structure and then increasing the volume of vocabularies. If a language is a building, then grammar is a plan and vocabularies are bricks. This book has been made to make the bricks available in your hands.

To grasp many vocabularies, the perception of the concept of the parts of speech should precede it. Only then, the functions in sentences can be grasped and the words learned once are not easily forgotten. In this context, the basic concept of Korean parts of speech was arranged on the beginning part of this dictionary.

In the article of vocabulary arrangement, 6,000 words selected by 'The National Academy of the Korean Language' have been re-classified in Korean alphabetic order with the notation A, B, C by the order of frequency. Readers who learn Korean as a hobby may be able to do basic conversations with only the 1,087 words of class A. The students who plan to study in Korea or to get jobs in Korea must know all of the 6,000 words.

Hope all of you will build a great house with diversified bricks termed vocabulary.

Explanatory Notes

1. Condensed the vocabulary to the 6,000 words selected by <The National Academy of the Korean Language> and arranged them in Korean alphabetic order. These are the words that any foreigner who studies Korean must inevitably know.

2. All entry words were classified as 3 classes as those for class A(1,087) that are most frequently used, class B(2,111) and class C(2,872) based on the order of frequent use and ones who mastered the words up to class C may apply 6th class of Korean language ability test.

3. By arranging all of the words based on their part of speech, this book focused on studying rather than referencing unlike existing dictionaries.

4. In the first part of this book, a short description of the relevant part of speech was presented to help understanding of the part of speech.

5. For nouns of '하다' type, added (하) next to the entry words to indicate that those may be used as verbs. ex)가능(可能)(하)

6. For words originated from the words written in Chinese characters, specified Chinese characters for Chinese and Japanese learners to remember easily. ex) 가격(價格)

7. In case there are multiple significances of a word, showed the explanations of different significances under numbers such as ❶, ❷.

8. For words originated from foreign languages, specified relevant foreign languages. ex) 가이드(guide)

9. In case the pronunciation of a word is different from the way it is written, specified the pronunciation in a [ ]. These phonetic transcriptions were based on easy pronunciation for foreigners.

10 The abbreviations are as follows.
   noun → ⓝ, pronoun → ⓞ
   numeral → ⓤ, verb → ⓥ
   supplementary verb → ⓢ, adjective → ⓐ
   pre-noun → ⓡ, adverb → ⓓ
   exclamation → ⓔ, abbreviation → abbr.

11 About Korean language ability test
   http://www.klpt.org
   http://www.kltkorea.com
   http://www.topik.or.kr

Korean
Essential
Vocabular y 6000

Any foreigner who studies
Korean must inevitably know

ㄱ_ 50   ㄴ_ 106   ㄷ_ 122   ㄹ_ 153   ㅁ_ 155
ㅂ_ 177   ㅅ_ 208   ㅇ_ 253   ㅈ_ 307   ㅊ_ 346
ㅋ_ 361   ㅌ_ 365   ㅍ_ 372   ㅎ_ 380

1. The grammatical characters and parts of speech of Korean

Ones who do not know their native languages can't learn foreign languages. That is, a minimum understanding of native language is required to learn other foreign languages well. In other words, learning a foreign language well means good perception of it's differences from the native language at the first stage. Now, let's review the differences of Korean from the native languages you know.

1 The grammatical characters of Korean

1 There are vowel harmony phenomena.

The vowels can be divided as positive vowels and negative vowels. Here, the phenomena that positive vowels(ㅏ · ㅑ · ㅗ · ㅛ) harmonize with each other and negative vowels(ㅓ · ㅕ · ㅜ · ㅠ) with each other is termed vowel harmony phenomena. Such phenomena are prominently apparent between echoic words and mimetic words or between the word stems and word tails.

ex) 펄럭펄럭, 찰싹찰싹, 얼룩덜룩, 깎아, 꺾어 등

❷ There are first sound rules.
  (1) 'ㄹ' or 'ㄴ' is avoided for the first sound of a word.
     ex) 력사→역사, 녀자→여자
  (2) In writing foreign languages in Korean letters, consonants are not piled up in the first sound thus 'ㅡ' sound is added.
     ex) strike→스트라이크, prime→프라임

❸ Modifiers precede the modified words.
  Modifiers precede the words to be modified to modify them.
  ex) fast go, nice person
      빨리 간다, 착한 사람

❹ The structure is 'subject+object+predicate'.
  Unlike English or Chinese, objects precede predicates in Korean.
  ex) I school go, Brother meal eat
      나는 학교에 간다, 동생이 밥을 먹는다.

❺ Adjectives are developed.
  Adjectives that describe shapes of things are quite developed. This is not easily found in other languages.
  ex) blue

파랗다, 파릇파릇하다, 파르스름하다

6 Respectful words are developed.

Diversified respectful words give headaches to foreign learners. But without proper use of respectful words, a good command of Korean language can't be achieved.

ex) 간다, 가시오, 가세요, 가십시오, 가시게, 가게, 가시지요(go)

7 Consonant assimilation(子音同化) phenomena are substantial.

This is the phenomenon that when a consonant at the end of a syllable meets the consonants succeeding, one of those two consonants assimilates another one and changes to similar or same sound as the other one or both of the consonants change to a sound.

ex) 밥물→밤물, 종로→종노, 섭리→섬니, 신라→실라

8 Many words were originated from words written in Chinese characters and words in foreign languages.

There are so many words originated from the words written in Chinese characters that those account for more than half of the words in Korean. Also, affected by western culture, the words originated from the words of western countries are quite widely used. This aspect may act somewhat beneficial to foreigners in acquisition of the words.

ex) 학교(學校), 정치(政治), 문화(文化), 컵(cup), 텔레비전(television)

⑨ There are lots of diversifications in declinable words.

Verbs and adjectives are used in basic forms in few cases and generate changes of the word tails based on the situations in most of the cases. We may recognize the patterns of sentences by the changes of the word tails.

  가다(basic form)
  갑니까?(questioning form)
  갑시다(requesting form)
  가시오(ordering form)
  가지 마십시오(prohibiting form)
  가면(presuming form)
  가도(conditioning form)
  갈수록(increasing form)
  가든지(selecting form)

⑩ Case auxiliary words are developed.

Although the basic word order of Korean is 'subject+object+predicate', the positioning is comparably free. It is because the case auxiliary word are developed. Chinese decides the sentence components based on the positioning but Korean decides the sentence compo-

nents by the case auxiliary words.
- subject case auxiliary words(이 / 가, 께서)
- object case auxiliary words(을 / 를)
- pre-noun case auxiliary word(의)
- adverb case auxiliary words (에, 에게, 께, 에게, 에게서)
- connective case auxiliary words (과 / 와, 하고)
- vocative case auxiliary words(아 / 야)
- auxiliary(은 / 는, 도, 마저, 부터)

2 Parts of speech in Korean

Parts of speech refer the categories of words that are the collections of the words of the same natures. Parts of speech are classified based on the functions, forms and significances of words. Korean words are generally classified as 9 parts of speech i. e. nouns, pronouns, numerals, verbs, adjectives, pre-nouns, adverbs, exclamations and auxiliary words. Then they are classified as substantives and expletives based on their independency and auxiliary words are the expletives and others are substantives. And words that are changeable of the forms are termed declinable words and words that are not changeable of the forms are termed uninflected words or embellishing words. Following is the table of the classifications.

Table of classification of parts of speech

basis of classification			
independency	form	function	significance
substantive (independent word)	un-changeable words	uninflected word	noun
			pronoun
			numeral
	changeable words	declinable word	verb
			adjective
	un-changeable words	embellishing word	pre-noun
			adverb
	un-changeable words	independent word	exclamation
expletive (dependent word)	-	connective word	auxiliary word

3 Grammatical terms that must be perceived

- 형태소(形態素): element of form
- 단어(單語): word
- 구(句): phrase
- 절(節): clause

- 문장(文章): sentence
- 글, 문단(文段): paragraph
- 문장성분(文章成分): components that compose a sentence

sentence components		
major components	sub-components	independency
subject	pre-noun words	independent words
predicate	adverb words	
object		
complement		

❶ subject

The word that is a doer of an action in a sentence. It consists of an uninflected word with an attached subject case auxiliary word at the end. In the sentence '하늘이(sky+auxiliary word) 높다(high).', '하늘' is the subject. The subjects are primarily nouns, pronouns and numerals.

❷ predicate

The word that describes action, status, nature etc of the subject in a sentence. In the sentence '장미가(rose+auxiliary word) 아름답다(beautiful)', '아름답다' is the predicate. The predicates are primarily verbs and adjectives.

❸ object

The word that is the object of an action or an effect expressed by a transitive verb in a sentence. It consists of an uninflected word with an attached object case auxiliary word at the end. In the sentence '책을(book+auxiliary word) 읽다(read)', '책' is the object. The objects are primarily nouns, pronouns and numerals.

❹ complement

In case the significance of a sentence is not sufficiently explained by a subject and a predicate in a sentence, a complement makes up for the insufficiency of the explanation. In case '되다(become)', '아니다(is not)', etc are the predicates, it is an essential sentence component. In the sentences '물이(water+auxiliary word) 얼음이(ice+auxiliary word) 되다(become).' and '그는(he+auxiliary word) 천재가(genius+auxiliary word) 아니다(is not)', '얼음이', '천재가' are the complements.

❺ pre-noun word

The word that embellishes the content of a substantive preceding the substantive in a sentence. In the sentence '예쁜(beautiful) 학생(student)', '예쁜' is the pre-noun.

⑥ adverb word

It defines primarily changeable words in sentences and in some cases defines pre-nouns, adverbs or whole sentences in sentences. In the sentence '몹시(very) 춥다(cold)', '몹시' is the adverb word.

⑦ independent word

The word that embellishes the whole sentence or a clause independently without direct connection with major component or sub-component of the sentence in a sentence. It consists of exclamations, terms of reference, designating words and connecting words, etc. In the sentence '이런(aha), 열쇠를(key+auxiliary word) 잃어버렸잖아(lost).', '이런' is the independent word.

⑧ word stem

The element of form that is not changed in inflections of changeable words.

ex) '잡다' · '잡아' · '잡으니'에서 '잡'[catch]

⑨ word tail

The part that is attached to the end of the stem of a declinable word or a predicate case auxiliary word and indicates grammatical context in various changeable forms based on the usage.

ex) 읽(stem)+다(tail) 읽(stem)+습니다.(tail) 읽

(stem)+습니까?(tail) 읽(stem)+을수록(tail)]
[read]

2 Noun

1 definition of noun
word that express name of a thing

2 characters of noun

1. The form is fixed and does not change.
2. It may be embellished by an pre-noun.

   새(new) 가방(bag)

   아름다운(beautiful) 아가씨(girl)

3. Attached by an auxiliary word, it is used as various kinds of sentence components.

   -Subject :
   이(this) 가방이(bag+auxiliary word) 무겁다(heavy).

   -predicate :
   이것은(this thing+auxiliary word) 누나의(sister+auxiliary word) 가방이다(bag+auxiliary word).

   -object :
   아버지가(father+auxiliary word) 새(new) 가방을(bag+auxiliary word) 사(buy) 오셨다(come+

auxiliary word).
-complement :
이것은(this+auxiliary word) <u>가방이</u>(bag+auxiliary word) 아니다(not+tail).
-pre-noun :
<u>가방의</u>(bag+auxiliary word) 끈이(webbing+auxiliary word) 떨어졌다(separate+tail).
-adverb word :
너의(you+auxiliary word) <u>가방에</u>(bag+auxiliary word) 담아라(put+tail).
-independent word :
<u>가방</u>(bag), 그것은(that+auxiliary word) 학생에게(student+auxiliary word) 꼭(definitely) 필요한(need+auxiliary word) 물건이다(thing+tail).

3 kinds of noun

1 based on the range of use

-common noun : A noun that generally express a name of a thing
ex) 학교(school), 사랑(love), 선생님(teacher)
-proper noun : A name referring a certain particular human or thing

ex) 동대문(Dongdaemun), 마이클(Michale),
　　중국(China), 삼국지(3 nations' story)

❷ Based on the existence or non- existence of independency

-independent noun : noun that is used not being helped by other words

ex) 동대문(Dongdaemun), 선생님(teacher),
　　사람(man)

-dependent noun : It is a noun by the nature but the significance is perfunctory thus depends on other words in use. It is also called incomplete noun.

ex) 분(sir), 뿐(only), 것(thing), 수(way),
　　데(place), 줄(case)

3 Pronoun

1 definition of pronoun
The word that indicates a person, a thing or a place on behalf of the names

2 characters of pronoun
1. The form is fixed and does not change.
2. Used as various kinds of sentence components with attached auxiliary words at the end.
3. pre-nouns preceding pronouns are quite limited.

착한(nice) 당신(you),

내가(I+auxiliary word) 읽던(read) 그것(that),

아무(something) 이것(this)(×)

3 kinds of pronoun
1. personal pronoun : pronouns that is used to indicate a persons
1st person: indicates the speaker(s)
ex) 나, 우리, 저, 저희-I or we

2nd person: indicates listener(s)
ex) 너, 너희, 자네, 그대, 당신-you
3rd person: indicates other(s)
ex) 이분, 저분, 그분, 이이, 저이, 그이, 누구, 아무
-he, she, they, who

❷ indicating pronoun : pronouns that indicate things or places classification

classification	thing pronoun	place pronoun
close indication	이것(this)	여기(here)
neutral indication	그것(it)	거기(there)
far indication	저것(that)	저기(there)
uncertain indication	무엇, 어느 것 (what, which)	어디(where)
unlimited indication	아무것(any)	아무데 (anywhere)

(1) 이, 그, 저

이, 그, 저 attached by auxiliary words or dependent nouns are pronouns and those without attachment are pre-nouns.

ex) 그가(he+auxiliary word) 온다. (come).
(pronoun)

저(that) 사람(person) (pre-noun)

(2) 이리, 그리, 저리

These are not pronouns but adverbs because auxiliary words can't be attached freely.

ex) 이리가(this way+auxiliary word)(×)
　　그리를(that way+auxiliary word)(×)

4 Numeral

1 definition of numeral
The word that indicates volume or order of things

2 characters of numeral
1. The forms are fixed and do not change.
2. Used as various kinds of sentence components attached by auxiliary words.
3. Can't be embellished by pre-nouns or uninflected word type declinable words.
   ex) 새 하나(×), 큰 둘(×)

3 kinds of numeral
1. volume numeral :
   numerals that indicate volumes
   (1) native words type : 하나, 둘, 셋, 넷, 다섯…
   (2) volume numeral-Chinese character word type : 일, 이, 삼, 사, 오, 육…
2. ordinal numeral :
   numerals that indicate order
   (1) native words type : 첫째, 둘째, 셋째, 넷째…
   (2) volume numeral-Chinese character word type : 제일, 제이, 제삼, 제사…

4. numeral and pre-noun

1. numeral : can be attached by auxiliary word.
   ex) 둘보다 <u>하나</u>가 적다.
2. pre-noun :
   followed by noun indicating unit.
   ex) 사과 <u>한</u> 개를 샀다.

5. numeral and pronoun

1. numeral : indicates an object in sentence.
   ex) 사과 <u>하나</u>를 샀다. (indicates '사과')
2. pronoun : indicates an object in a place out of the sentence.
   ex) 철수가 거기에 있다. ('거기'is not present in the sentence)

❋ As for uninflected word

1. definition of uninflected word : The word that indicates collection of noun, pronoun and numeral
2. characters of uninflected word
   (1) primarily used as major components of sentences.
   (2) The form is fixed and does not change.

(3) Does various functions attached by an auxiliary word in a sentence.
(4) Embellished by pre-noun.
 -noun : can be embellished by pre-noun and indeclinable adjective type word.
 -pronoun : can be embellished by only pre-noun type word.
 -numeral : can't be embellished by neither pre-noun nor pre-noun type word.

❸ plural number of uninflected word

attaches tail word '들' at the end of countable noun or pronoun to indicate plural number.

ex) <u>학생들</u>이 운동장에 있다.

5 Verb

1 definition of verb
The words that indicate actions or phenomena of things

2 characters of verb
1. actions : movements of humans
   ex) 가다, 오다, 노래하다, 사랑하다, 생각하다
2. phenomena : movement of the nature
   ex) 뜨다, 새다, 흐르다, 피다, 죽다, 늙다, 닮다

3 definition of declinable words
The words that have the function to describe the subject of sentences and consist of verbs and adjectives.

4 characters of declinable words
1. The forms are changed based on the usages.
2. primarily used as predicates in sentences.
3. can be divided as word stem that indicates the meaning and tail of word that indicates grammatical relationship.

5 inflection of declinable words

1. **inflection** : the changes of the form of a word by attachment of various word tails at the end of a word stem
   (1) word stem : the part that does not change in inflection. It carries the meaning of the word.
   (2) word tail : the part that changes in inflection. It indicates grammatical relationship.
   (3) basic type : words composed by word stems attached by the word tail '-다'. used as entry words in dictionaries.

2. **inflecting word**
   words that inflect. Verb, adjective and predicate case auxiliary word belong to this.

   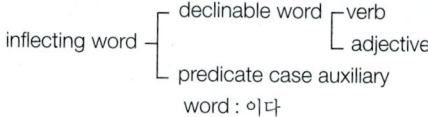

3. **types of inflection**
   (1) completing type: type that completes sentences.
   There are plain predicating type, questioning type, ordering type, requesting type, exclaiming type.
   ex) 철수가 <u>간다</u>. 철수가 <u>가냐</u>? 철수야, <u>가거</u>

라. 철수야, 가자. 철수가 <u>가는구나</u>.
(2) connecting type: type that connects sentences.

There are equivalent, subordinating, assisting types.

ex) 비가 <u>오고</u>, 바람이 분다. 비가 <u>오면</u>, 꽃이 핀다. 비가 <u>오고</u> 있다.

(3) transforming type: type that transforms func-tions of sentences. There are noun type and pre-noun type.

ex) 집에 <u>가기</u>가 어렵다.
집에 <u>가는</u> 차가 몇 번이냐?

❹ about predicate case auxiliary word '-이다'
  (1) attaches to uninflected words to make them predicating words.
  (2) '-이다' of '-이-' can be omitted.
      ex) 그것은 소(이)다.
  (3) The form of inflection is similar to adjective but sometimes '로' may be added.
      ex) 이제는 가을<u>이로군</u>.

❺ forms of inflection

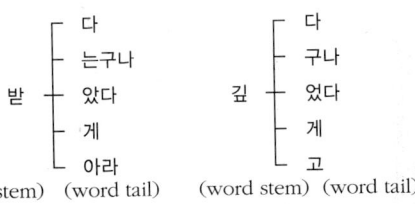

6 identification of word stem and word tail
  (1) If the word tail '-게' is attached, most of the word stems become apparent.
    ex) <u>흐르</u>게, <u>먹</u>게, <u>올</u>게
  (2) The '-시' for respecting is deemed to be word tail.
  (3) Balance after excluding word stem is word tail.
    ex) 가셨다 → 가(시)겠 (You can see that '가-' is the word stem.)
    therefore, 가셨다 = 가+셨다.

7 classification of inflection
  (1) Completing types come only at the end of sentences.
  (2) inflection types appear in the middle of sentences are connecting type and transforming type. Between these, the ones except transforming type are connecting type.

6. Adjective

1. definition of adjective
The words that indicate nature or status of things

2. kinds of adjective
1. nature status adjective - The adjective that indicate nature or status
   (1) nature(objective adjective) : can't be attached by '아/어하다'
   ex) 꽃이 붉다. (→꽃이 붉어한다.(×))
   (2) status(subjective adjective) : can be attached by '아/어하다'
   ex) 나는 배고프다. (→나는 배고파한다.(○))
2. demonstrative adjective : The adjective that has the nature of denoting
   ex) 이러하다, 저러하다, 그러하다

3. distinguishment between verb and adjective
Both verb and adjective change their forms thus have basic form that is the form of 'stem+다'. There only verb and adjective have basic form among the parts of speech.

① If a word is attched by '-ㄴ다/-는다', it is a verb.
Try to attach '-는다', '-ㄴ다'
먹다 - 먹는다(○) → verb
높다 - 높는다(×) → adjective
그리다 - 그린다(○) → verb
그립다 - 그립는다(×) → adjective

② If a word can complete predication by only basic form, it is an adjective.
밥을 <u>먹다</u>.(×) → verb
꽃이 <u>아름답다</u>.(○) → adjective

③ '-아라/어라' are used as ordering type with verbs and as exclaiming type in adjectives.
밥을 <u>먹어라</u>.(drdering) → verb
산이 <u>높아라</u>.(exclaiming) → adjective

Try to attach ordering type word tails '-아라', '-어라'.
먹다 - 먹어라(○) → verb
그리다 - 그려라(○) → verb
높다 - 높아라(×) → adjective
그립다 - 그리워라(×) → adjective
(This is possible for exclaiming form.)

7 Pre-noun

1 definition of pre-noun
The words that come before uninflected words to embellish the uninflected words in detail

2 characters of pre-noun
1. form is fixed and does not inflect.
2. no auxiliary word is attached in any case.
3. used as an uninflected word in a sentence.
4. as an independent part of speech, written with spaces to other words.

3 types of pre-nouns
1. nature status pre-noun : the pre-noun that embellishes nature or status of an uninflected word
   ex) 새, 헌, 첫, 옛, 윗, 뒷, 온, 뭇, 한, 온갖, 갖은, 외딴, 오른, 왼, 참, 거짓……
2. demonstrative pre-noun : the pre-noun that has de noting nature
   ex) 이, 그, 저, 요, 고, 조, 이런, 저런, 그런, 무슨, 어느, 딴, 아무……

③ **numeral pre-noun** : the pre-noun that indicates the volume of the succeeding noun
ex) 한, 두, 세(석), 네(넉), 다섯, 여섯, 일, 이, 삼, 반, 전(全), 총(總)……

4 pre-noun and pre-noun form of declinable word

① pre-noun
  (1) can't indicate tense. ex) 새 (no tense)
  (2) can't inflect.
  (3) is the pre-noun part of speech.
  (4) can only embellish.

② pre-noun form of declinable word
  (1) can indicate tense.
   ex) 새로운(the present), 새로울(the future)
  (2) is inflected type of declinable word.
  (3) is not the pre-noun part of speech.
  (4) can embellish and also predicate.

5 pre-noun word and pre-noun

① pre-noun word : the sentence component that embellish uninflected word
② pre-noun : among the pre-noun words, the words that do not either combine with auxiliary words or change the word tails

example	component	part of speech
새 집	pre-noun	pre-noun word
<u>나의</u> 집	pronoun+ auxiliary word	pre-noun word
<u>높은</u> 집	word stem+ word tail	pre-noun word

6 the part of speech of '다른'

① if it predicates → adjective
  ex) 이것과 저것은 <u>다른</u> 책이다. (the predicate of '저것은')

② if it does not predicate → pre-noun
  ex) <u>다른</u> 책을 보자.

7 pre-noun and prefix

① pre-noun : independent word, written with space from uninflected word ex) <u>새</u> 책

② prefix : because dependent should not be written with space ex) <u>맨</u>손

8 Adverb

1 definition of adverb

The words that embellish primarily uninflected words to make the meaning more clear. Mimetic words and echoic words are also adverbs.

2 characters of adverb

1. The form is fixed and does not inflect.
2. can use supplementary auxiliary word.
3. primarily embellishes declinable words but can operate multiple other functions.
4. is primarily adverb word in sentence but serves as an independent word in case of connecting sentences.

3 types of adverbs

1. component adverbs: the adverbs that primarily embellish a component of sentences
   (1) nature status adverbs: adverbs that indicate conditions or extents
   (2) demonstrative adverbs: adverbs that denote places, times or facts, etc in sentences
   (3) denying adverbs: adverbs that embellish

the contents of in-declinable words in the manner to deny

❷ sentence adverbs : adverbs that embellish whole sentences
   (1) mode adverbs: adverbs that indicate the attitudes of speakers which determine about whole sentences
   ex) 잘, 급히, 가만히, 일찍, 이미, 갑자기, 너무, 퐁당, 출렁출렁, 옹기종기……
   (2) demonstrative adverb: adverbs that connect components and sentences
   ex) 이리, 저리, 그리, 오늘, 내일, 어제……
   (3) denying adverb
   ex) 아니(안), 못……
   (4) mode adverb
   ex) 과연, 설마, 만약, 제발, 진실로, 정녕……
   (5) connecting adverb
   ex) 그리고, 그러나, 및, 또는, 왜냐하면……

❹ functions of adverbs

❶ embellish uninflected words.
   ex) 글씨를 빨리 쓴다.(verb)

강이 <u>매우</u> 깊다. (adjective)

② embellish pre-noun and adverb.
   ex) <u>몹시</u> 헌 책이다. (pre-noun)

   <u>매우</u> 빨리 달린다. (adverb)

③ also embellish uninflected words.
   ex) <u>조금</u> 뒤에 보자. (noun)

   <u>바로</u> 그가 범인이다. (pronoun)

   <u>겨우</u> 하나를 만들었다. (numeral)

④ also embellish phrase or clause.
   ex) <u>오로지</u> <u>그의 덕택으로</u> 살았다. (phrase)

⑤ sometimes embellish whole sentences.
   ex) <u>제발</u>, <u>그만 두십시오</u>. (sentence)

9 Exclamation

1 definition of exclamation
The words that indicate speaker's calling, feeling, fright or answer

2 characters of exclamation
1. The form is fixed and does not inflect.
2. not attached by an auxiliary word and becomes an independent word in a sentence.
3. primarily comes in front of a sentence but some times can be in the middle or at the end of the sentence.

3 types of exclamations
1. emotion ex) 아, 아차, 아하, 허허, 아이고, 에끼, 아무렴……
2. will ex) 어라, 자, 천만에, 옳지, 좋다, 그렇지, 옛다……
3. call ex) 여보, 여보세요, 여보게, 얘……
4. answer ex) 예, 그래, 오냐, 글쎄, 글쎄올시다……

4 comparison among pre-noun, adverb and exclamation

① common characters
(1) the forms are fixed and do not change.
(2) independent parts of speech written with space from other words.
(3) do one function in sentence.

② differences
(1) pre-noun
  ① embellish uninflected words
  ② can't take auxiliary word.
  ③ always used depending on uninflected words.
  ④ sentence component is pre-noun word.

(2) adverb
  ① embellish declinable words.
  ② may take auxiliary word.
  ③ may form a sentence on it's own.
  ④ used as adverb words or independent words.

(3) exclamation
  ① independent in sentence.
  ② can't take auxiliary word.
  ③ may form a sentence on it's own.
  ④ always used as independent words in sentences.

5 identification of exclamation

1. can't be attached by auxiliary word in principle.
2. is in the form of 'uninflected word+auxiliary word', but the forms fixed as one word are deemed as exclamations.
   ex) 정말로(정말 + 로), 애(이 아이야),
   웬걸(웬 것을), 뭐(무엇)
3. The sound that calls the other by actual name is not an exclamation.
   ex) 철수야, 학교에 가자.
4. presenting words or entry words at the beginning of sentences are not exclamations.
   ex) 연필, 그것은 꼭 필요한 학용품이다.
5. the sounds such as '구구(sound calling chickens), 이랴(sound driving cows) that call animals are exclamations.
6. In general, If a noun indicates the speaker's fright or feeling being used on behalf of a sentence, the noun becomes a exclamation.
   ex) 불!(불이 났다.)

10 Auxiliary word

1 definition of auxiliary word
The word that is attached to uninflected word and reveals the meaning of serving the role of uninflected word in the sentence.

2 characters of auxiliary words
1. Because of no independency, is attached to the end of words in using.
2. is primarily attached to uninflected words and serves the role of indicating grammatic relations or supplementing meanings.
3. can combine with connecting word tails of ad verbs or declinable words or other auxiliary words.

3 types of auxiliary words
1. case auxiliary words
   (1) The words that are attached to declinable words to reveal the meanings of the uninflected words serving the roles of uninflected words.

   subject case auxiliary words :The auxiliary

words that indicate the role as subjects
이 / 가, 께서, 에서(group), 서(human)
ex) 철수가 학교에 간다.

(2) object case auxiliary words :The auxiliary words that indicate the roles as object words
을 / 를 / ㄹ ex) 앞을 똑바로 보아라.

(3) complement case auxiliary words :The auxiliary words that indicate the roles as complements
이 / 가 ex) 그는 학생이 아니다.

(4) predicate case auxiliary words :The auxiliary words that indicate the roles as predicating words
이다 ex) 영희는 학생이다.

(5) pre-noun case auxiliary words :The auxiliary words that indicate the roles as pre-noun words
의 ex) 순이의 옷은 매우 예쁘다.

(6) adverb case auxiliary words :The auxiliary words that indicate the roles as adverb
에, 에서, 에게 께, 한테, (으)로, (으)로서, (으)로써, 처럼, 같이, 만큼, 보다, 라고

ex) 이 책을 너<u>에게</u> 주마.
(7) vocative case auxiliary word: The auxiliary words that make to become the objectives of calling
아/야, (이)여, (이)시여 ex) 철수<u>야</u>, 학교에 가자.

❷ complementing auxiliary words : The auxiliary words that do not define uninflected words to certain cases but are generally used for the components of sentences to add special meanings of the words
ex) 은/는(subject, contrasting), 도(also), 만(the only), 조차(also, even), 부터(beginning, first), 까지(arrival), (이)나 (selection), 마저 (even, also), 밖에(not any more), 뿐(only)

❸ connecting auxiliary words : The auxiliary words that serve the roles of connecting two words with equivalent qualification
와 / 과, (이)며, (이)고, 랑, 에다
ex) 철수<u>와</u> 순이는 학생이다.

4 attachments of auxiliary words

❶ auxiliary words are primarily attached to uninflected words.
ex) 배<u>가</u> 빨리 달린다. 우리<u>는</u> 산<u>을</u> 좋아한다.

❷ also attached to adverbs, adverb case auxiliary words or connecting word tails of declinable words.

ex) 오늘은 날씨가 몹시도 나쁘다.
(adverb+auxiliary word)
ex) 서울에서는 별을 보기가 매우 힘들다. (adverb case auxiliary word+auxiliary word)
ex) 그것은 마음에 들지가 않는다. (connecting word tail+auxiliary word)

❸ auxiliary words can combine each other.
(1) case auxiliary word + complementing auxiliary word ex) 나에게는 쉽지 않다.
(2) complementing auxiliary word +case auxiliary word ex) 철수까지가 합격이다.
(3) complementing auxiliary word +complementing auxiliary word
ex) 그 책만은 보지 말아라.

5 transformation of auxiliary words

Some of the auxiliary words transform based on preceding sounds, whether they are vowels or consonants.

❶ consonant + 이, 을, 아, 으로, 은, 과······
❷ vowel + 가, 를, 야, 로, 는, 와······
ex) 순이는 사과와 밤을 샀다.
아버님은 밤과 사과를 사셨다.

6 auxiliary words and words

Words originally indicate things that work independently but the auxiliary words that can be easily separated from independent form elements are deemed as words. Therefore the auxiliary words are the only words that are attached to preceding words to be used.

types of adverb case auxiliary words

① place : 에, 에서 ex) 학교에 있다.
② grant : 에, 에게, 께, 한테 ex) 동생에게 주었다.
③ taking : 에서, 에게서, 한테서
   ex) 형님에게서 받았다.
④ origin : 에서, 서 ex) 서울에서 오다.
⑤ directing : 에, (으)로, 에게로 ex) 바다로 가자.
⑥ cause : (으)로, 에 ex) 불에 타다.
⑦ tool : (으)로, (으)로써 ex) 칼로써 연필을 깎다.
⑧ qualification : (으)로, (으)로서
   ex) 학생으로서 할 일
⑨ common, comparison : 와, 과, 하고, 랑
⑩ comparison : 처럼, 같이, 만큼, 보다
⑪ quotation : 고, 라고

⑦ case indications of complementing auxiliary words

As complementing auxiliary words appear on the positions of various kinds of cases, thus try to reveal original cases to determine sentence components.

❶ 우리도 자유를 원한다.
  ⇒ 우리가 자유를 원한다. (subject case)
❷ 우리가 책도 샀다.
  ⇒ 우리가 책을 샀다. (object case)

8 functions of '와/과'

auxiliary words '와/과' are used in two irregularity.

❶ 철수와 순이는 학생이다.
  (connecting auxiliary word)
❷ 순이는 철수와 다르다.
  (adverb case auxiliary word)

In case '와/과' appear in front of subject words(or object words) like ❶, they are connection auxiliary words and if they are at the of subject words(or object words) ike ❷, they are adverb case auxiliary words.

9 omission of the auxiliary words

❶ appears on in spoken style.
❷ appears in case the case of the uninflected word is clear on it's own.

ㄱ

A	ⓝ 가게	store
B	ⓝ 가격(價格)	price
B	ⓝ 가구(家具)	furniture
C	ⓝ 가구(家口)	family
B	ⓥ 가까워지다	get in with (a person), get near (a place)
B	ⓝⓓ 가까이	vicinity/near
A	ⓐ 가깝다[-따]	❶(be) near ❷(be) familiar ❸(be) similar
B	ⓥ 가꾸다	❶take care of (plants) ❷decorate (the interior)
A	ⓓ 가끔	occasionally
C	ⓝ 가난(하)	poverty
B	ⓐ 가난하다	(be) poor
B	ⓐ 가늘다	(be) thin

C	ⓝ 가능(可能)(하)	possibility
B	ⓝ 가능성(可能性)[-썽]	possibility
B	ⓐ 가능하다(可能-)	(be) possible
C	ⓥ 가능해지다(可能-)	become possible
A	ⓥ 가다	❶ go
		❷ (time) pass
		❸ blow out
		❹ go bad
A	ⓢ 가다	…ing
B	ⓓ 가득	all filled
B	ⓐ 가득하다[-드카-]	(be) full
C	ⓓ 가득히[-드키]	to the full
C	ⓥ 가라앉다[-안따]	❶ sink
		❷ become quiet
		❸ get calm
C	ⓥ 가려지다	be covered
C	ⓓ 가령(假令)	supposing
B	ⓝ 가로	width
C	ⓝ 가로등(街路燈)	streetlight
C	ⓥ 가로막다[-따]	interrupt
C	ⓝ 가로수(街路樹)	trees lining a street

B n	가루	powder
C v	가르다	divide
A v	가르치다	teach
C n	가르침	lesson
B v	가리다	❶ distinguish ❷ be shy of strangers
B v	가리다	cover
B v	가리키다	indicate
C d	가만	just as it is
C v	가만있다[-마닏따]	remain quiet
B d	가만히	calmly
C n	가뭄	drought
A n	가방	bag
A a	가볍다[-따]	(be) light\<weight\>
C n	가사	lyrics
C n	가상(假想)(하)	imagination
A n	가수(歌手)	singer
B n	가스(gas)	❶ fluid ❷ gas
A n	가슴	❶ chest ❷ mind
B n	가슴속[-쏙]	one's heart

B	n 가요(歌謠)	popular song
A	n 가운데	❶middle ❷among
B	n 가위	scissors
A	n 가을	autumn
B	n 가이드(guide)	guide
C	n 가입(加入)(하)	joining
C	n 가입자(加入者)[-짜]	subscriber
C	v 가입하다[-이파-]	join
A	d 가장	extremely
C	n 가장(家長)	patriarch
B	n 가정(家庭)	household
C	n 가정(假定)(하)	assumption
C	n 가정교사(家庭敎師)	tutor
B	v 가져가다	take
B	v 가져다주다	bring
A	v 가져오다	bring
A	n 가족(家族)	❶members of a family ❷family
B	n 가죽	leather
B	n 가지	kind

B	n 가지	branch
A	s 가지다	from;with;by means of
A	v 가지다	①take, carry ②have, possess
B	n 가짜	①fake ②forgery
C	n 가치(價値)	value
C	n 가치관(價値觀)	one's values
C	n 가톨릭(Catholic)	①Roman Catholicism ②Roman Catholic
C	v 가하다(加-)	①give ②increase
B	r 각(各)	①each ②every kind of
B	d 각각(各各)[-깍]	each
B	n 각각(各各)[-깍]	each
B	n 각국(各國)[-꾹]	each nation
C	d 각기(各其)[-끼]	each
C	n 각오(覺悟)(하)[가고]	resolution
B	nd 각자(各自)[-짜]	each one /individually

B	ⓝ 각종(各種)[-쫑]	all kinds
C	ⓝ 간	saltiness
C	ⓝ 간(肝)	liver
B	ⓝ 간(間)	interval
C	ⓝ 간격(間隔)	❶ space
		❷ estrangement
B	ⓐ 간단하다(簡單-)	(be) simple
B	ⓓ 간단히(簡單-)	easily
C	ⓝ 간부(幹部)	executive
C	ⓝ 간섭(干涉)(하)	interfere
B	ⓝ 간식(間食)	between-meal-snack
C	ⓓ 간신히(艱辛-)	barely
B	ⓝ 간장(-醬)	soy sauce
C	ⓝ 간접(間接)	indirectness
C	ⓝ 간접적(間接的)[-쩍]	indirect
C	ⓝ 간판(看板)	signboard
C	ⓐ 간편하다(簡便-)	(be) convenient
C	ⓝ 간호(看護)(하)	nursing
A	ⓝ 간호사(看護師)	nurse
C	ⓓ 간혹(間或)	sometimes

C	v 갇히다[가치-]	be locked in
B	v 갈다	change
B	v 갈다	❶ sharpen
		❷ gnash (one's teeth)
C	n 갈등(葛藤)[-뜽]	conflict
A	n 갈비	rib
B	n 갈비탕	beef-rip soup
B	n 갈색(褐色)[-쌕]	brown
C	d 갈수록[-쑤-]	as time goes by
B	v 갈아입다[가라-따]	change one's clothes
B	v 갈아타다[가라-]	change cars, trains
C	n 갈증(渴症)[-쯩]	thirst
B	n 감	persimmon
C	n 감(感)	feeling
C	n 감각(感覺)(하)	sense
A	n 감기(感氣)	influenza
C	v 감다[-따]	roll up (a muffler)
B	v 감다[-따]	close (one's eyes)
C	n 감독(監督)(하)	❶ supervision
		❷ director

56

B	ⓝ 감동(感動)(하)	strong impression
C	ⓝ 감동적(感動的)	impressive
A	ⓝ 감사(感謝)(하)	thanks
A	ⓥⓐ 감사하다(感謝-)	thank/(be) grateful
B	ⓝ 감상(鑑賞)(하)	appreciation
B	ⓥ 감상하다(鑑賞-)	appreciate
C	ⓝ 감소(減少)(하)	decrease
C	ⓥ 감소되다(減少-)	decrease
C	ⓥ 감소하다(減少-)	decrease
C	ⓝ 감수성(感受性)[-썽]	sensitivity
C	ⓥ 감싸다	wrap
C	ⓝ 감옥(監獄)[가목]	prison
B	ⓝ 감자	potato
B	ⓝ 감정(感情)	emotion
C	ⓝ 감정적(感情的)	emotional
C	ⓥ 감추다	❶hide ❷shelter
C	ⓓ 감히(敢-)	daringly
C	ⓝ 갑(匣)	tiny case (for cigarette or matches)
A	ⓓ 갑자기[-짜-]	suddenly

C	ⓐ 갑작스럽다[-짝쓰-따]	(be) sudden
A	ⓝ 값[갑]	❶ price ❷ value
C	ⓐ 값싸다[갑-]	(be) cheap
A	ⓝ 강(江)	river
C	ⓝ 강남(江南)	the south of a river
B	ⓝ 강당(講堂)	❶ lecture hall
		❷ Buddhist sanctum
C	ⓝ 강도(强度)	❶ intensity
		❷ solidity
B	ⓝ 강도(强盜)	burglar
C	ⓐ 강력하다(强力-)[-녀카-]	(be) powerful
C	ⓓ 강력히(强力-)[-녀키]	strongly
C	ⓐ 강렬하다(强烈-)[강녈-]	(be) intense
B	ⓝ 강물(江-)	river water
C	ⓝ 강변(江邊))	riverside
C	ⓝ 강북(江北)	the north of a river
C	ⓝ 강사(講師)	❶ lecturer
		❷ speaker
C	ⓝ 강수량(降水量)	rainfall
B	ⓝ 강아지	puppy
C	ⓥ 강요하다(强要-)	compel

58

B	ⓝ 강원도(江原道)	Gangwon-do
C	ⓝ 강의(講義)(하)[-이]	❶ instruction
		❷ a lecture
C	ⓥ 강의하다(講義-)[-이-]	lecture
B	ⓝ 강제(强制)(하)	compel
C	ⓝ 강조(强調)(하)	emphasis
B	ⓥ 강조하다(强調-)	emphasize
B	ⓐ 강하다(强-)	❶ (be) robust
		❷ (be) strong
C	ⓥ 강화하다(强化-)	strengthen
C	ⓝ 갖가지[갇까-]	all sorts of things
B	ⓥ 갖다[갇따]	❶ take
		❷ have, own
B	ⓢ 갖다[갇따]	❶ carry ❷ have
C	ⓥ 갖추다[갇-]	❶ furnish
		❷ possess
A	ⓐ 같다[갇따]	❶ (be) same
		❷ (be) identical
		❸ (be) alike
A	ⓓ 같이[가치]	together
C	ⓥ 같이하다[가치-]	❶ share

❷ be the same

C [v] 갚다[갑따] ❶ repay (a favor) ❷ retrun (a favor)

A [n] 개 ❶ dog ❷ cat's-paw

A [n] 개(個) unit or piece

C [n] 개개인(個個人) ❶ individual ❷ everyone

B [n] 개구리 frog

C [n] 개국(個國) countries

B [n] 개나리 forsythia <a kind of flower>

C [v] 개다 ❶ clear up<weather> ❷ soften with water ❸ fold (up)

C [n] 개미 ant

C [v] 개발되다(開發–) be developed

B [v] 개발하다(開發–) develop

C [n] 개방(開放)(하) opening

C [v] 개방되다(開放–) be opened

C [v] 개방하다(開放–) open (to the public)

C [n] 개별(個別) individual case

C	ⓝ 개선(改善)(하)	improvement
C	ⓥ 개선되다(改善-)	be improved
C	ⓥ 개선하다(改善-)	improve
C	ⓝ 개성(個性)	personality
A	ⓝ 개월(個月)	months
B	ⓝ 개인(個人)	private person
B	ⓝ 개인적(個人的)	private
C	ⓝ 객관적(客觀的)[-꽌-]	objective
A	ⓞ 거	abbr. of that place
A	ⓞ 거기	that place
C	ⓓ 거꾸로	backward
C	ⓐ 거대하다(巨大-)	(be) huge
C	ⓥ 거두다	❶ gather (cereals) ❷ gain or achieve ❸ remove ❹ look after (children) ❺ tidy up one's appearance
C	ⓥ 거들다	❶ help ❷ meddle

		or interfere
C	d 거듭	repeatedly
B	n 거리	a group of 50 <cucumbers, egg apple>
A	n 거리	street
C	n 거리(距離)	distance
C	v 거부하다(拒否-)	❶reject ❷deny
B	n 거실(居室)	living room
C	n 거액(巨額)	a big sum (of money)
A	n 거울	❶mirror ❷model or paragon ❸instruction
B	d 거의[-이]	hardly
C	v 거절하다(拒絕-)	refuse
B	n 거짓[-짇]	falsehood
B	n 거짓말[-진-]	lie
C	v 거치다	❶pass, undergo ❷graze

C	ⓐ 거칠다	❶ (be) rough
		❷ (be) harsh
		❸ (be) wild
		❹ (be) rude
C	ⓝ 거품	foam
A	ⓝ 걱정(하)[-쩡]	anxiety
B	ⓥ 걱정되다[-쩡-]	worry
B	ⓐ 걱정스럽다[-쩡-따]	(be) worried
A	ⓥ 걱정하다[-쩡-]	worry
C	ⓝ 건(件)	❶ case or matter
		❷ unit of case
A	ⓝ 건강(健康)(하)	health
A	ⓐ 건강하다(健康-)	(be) healthy
C	ⓝ 건너	the other side
B	ⓥ 건너가다	go over
B	ⓥ 건너다	❶ cross
		❷ ferry (by boat)
		❸ be carried <rumor>
B	ⓥ 건너오다	come over
B	ⓝ 건너편(-便)	the other side
C	ⓝ 건넛방(-房)[건너빵]	a room across from

		the main living room
C	ⓥ 건네다	❶ speak to ❷ ferry ❸ transfer (right, duty)
C	ⓥ 건네주다	hand over
C	ⓥ 건드리다	❶ touch ❷ offend
A	ⓝ 건물(建物)	building
C	ⓝ 건설(建設)	construction
C	ⓥ 건설되다(建設-)	construct
C	ⓥ 건설하다(建設-)	construct
C	ⓐ 건전하다(健全-)	(be) wholesome or sound
C	ⓝ 건조(乾燥)(하)	dryness
C	ⓐ 건조하다(乾燥-)	(be) dry
B	ⓥ 건지다	❶ pick up (in the liquid) ❷ rescue
B	ⓝ 건축(建築)(하)	architecture
C	ⓝ 걷기[-끼]	walking
A	ⓥ 걷다[-따]	walk

C [v] 걷다[-따]		❶collect (money) ❷roll up ❸remove
C [v] 걷다[-따]		roll up (one's sleeves)
A [v] 걸다		❶hang (a thing on a peg) ❷lock (the door) ❸hold ❹put up
B [v] 걸리다		❶be suspended (from) ❷be stuck ❸need
A [v] 걸어가다[거러-]		go on foot
A [v] 걸어오다[거러-]		come on foot
B [n] 걸음[거름]		walking
C [v] 걸치다		throw on or slip on
B [a] 검다[-따]		❶(be) black ❷(be) wicked
C [n] 검사(檢事)		prosecutor
B [n] 검사(檢査)(하)		inspection
A [n] 검은색(-色)[거든-]		black

B	n	검정색	black
C	n	검토(檢討)(하)	investigation
B	n	겁(怯)	fear
C	v	겁나다(怯-)[검-]	get scared
A	n	것[걷]	thing
B	n	겉[걷]	surface
C	n	게	crab
B	d	게다가	❶ there
			❷ besides
C	n	게시판(揭示板)	bulletin board
C	a	게으르다	(be) lazy
A	n	게임(game)(하)	game
B	d	겨우	❶ barely
			❷ at most
A	n	겨울	winter
B	n	겨울철	wintertime
C	n	겨자	❶ mustard <plant>
			❷ mustard <seasoning>
C	v	겪다[격따]	undergo
B	v	견디다	endure

C	n 견해(見解)	opinion
B	n 결과(結果)	consequence
C	n 결과적(結果的)	consequent
B	n 결국(結局)	termination
C	n 결론(結論)	conclusion
C	n 결석(缺席)(하)[-썩]	absence
C	v 결석하다(缺席)[-써카-]	be absent (from)
C	n 결승(決勝)(하)[-쏭]	the finals
C	n 결심(決心)(하)[-씸]	resolution
B	v 결심하다(決心-)[-씸-]	resolve
B	n 결정(決定)(하)[-쩡]	decision
B	v 결정되다(決定-)[-쩡-]	be decided
B	v 결정하다(決定-)[-쩡-]	decide
C	d 결코(決-)	never
A	n 결혼(結婚)(하)	marriage
A	n 결혼식(結婚式)	a wedding ceremony
A	v 결혼하다(結婚-)	marry
C	n 경계(境界)[-게]	boundary
C	n 경고(警告)(하)	warning
C	v 경고하다(警告-)	warn

C [n]	경기(景氣)	business conditions
B [n]	경기(競技)	contest
B [n]	경기도(京畿道)	Gyeonggi-do
B [n]	경기장(競技場)	stadium
C [n]	경력(經歷)[-녁]	career
A [n]	경복궁(景福宮)	Gyeongbokgung
C [n]	경비(經費)	expenses or expenditure
B [n]	경상도(慶尙道)	Gyeongsang-do
B [n]	경영(經營)(하)	management
C [v]	경영하다(經營-)	manage
B [n]	경우(境遇)	case or situation
C [n]	경쟁(競爭)(하)	competition
C [n]	경쟁력(競爭力)[-녁]	competitive power
B [n]	경제(經濟)	economy
C [n]	경제력(經濟力)	economic power
B [n]	경제적(經濟的)	❶ economic ❷ economical
C [n]	경제학(經濟學)	economics
A [n]	경주(慶州)	Gyeongju
A [n]	경찰(警察)	the police

A	n	경찰관(警察官)	policeman
A	n	경찰서(警察署)[-써]	police station
A	n	경치(景致)	scenery
C	n	경향(傾向)	trend
B	n	경험(經驗)(하)	experience
B	v	경험하다(經驗-)	experience
B	n	곁[견]	vicinity
C	n	계곡(溪谷)[게-]	valley
B	n	계단(階段)[게-]	stairs
A	n	계란(鷄卵)[게-]	egg
B	n	계산(計算)(하)[게-]	calculation
B	n	계산기(計算器)[게-]	calculator
B	v	계산하다(計算-)[게-]	calculate
A	d	계속(繼續)[게-]	continually
B	v	계속되다(繼續-)[게-]	continue
B	v	계속하다[-게소카-]	continue
A	s	계시다[게-]	(someone esteemed) be
A	v	계시다[게-]	honorific of be (of person)
B	n	계약(契約)(하)[게-]	contract

A	ⓝ 계절(季節)[계-]	season
C	ⓝ 계좌(計座)[계-]	(bank) account
C	ⓝ 계층(階層)[계-]	social stratum
A	ⓝ 계획(計劃)(하)[게-]	plan
B	ⓥ 계획하다(計劃-)[게회카-]	plan
B	ⓝ 고개	❶ occiput ❷ head
C	ⓝ 고개	❶ ridge ❷ crest or peak
B	ⓝ 고객(顧客)	customer
B	ⓝ 고교(高校)	abbr. of high school
C	ⓝ 고구려(高句麗)	Koguryeo (one of ancient nations)
B	ⓝ 고구마	sweet potato
C	ⓝ 고궁(古宮)	ancient palace
B	ⓝ 고급(高級)	high rank
C	ⓐ 고급스럽다(高級-)[-쓰-따]	(be) advanced
A	ⓝ 고기	meat
A	ⓝ 고등학교(高等學校)[-꾜]	high school
A	ⓝ 고등학생(高等學生)[-쌩]	hish school student
C	ⓝ 고려(高麗)	Koryeo

B	ⓥ 고려하다(考慮-)	consider
B	ⓥ 고르다	choose
B	ⓐ 고르다	(be) regular
A	ⓐ 고맙다[-따]	(be) thankful
B	ⓝ 고모(姑母)	a sister of one's father
B	ⓝ 고모부(姑母夫)	the husband of one's paternal aunt
C	ⓝ 고무신	rubber shoes
B	ⓝ 고민(苦悶)(하)	anguish
B	ⓥ 고민하다(苦悶-)	be in agony
B	ⓝ 고생(苦生)(하)	❶ sufferance ❷ hardship
B	ⓥ 고생하다(苦生-)	suffer
C	ⓐ 고소하다	❶ (be) tasty ❷ (be) jolly
B	ⓝ 고속(高速)	high speed
B	ⓝ 고속도로(高速道路)	express highway
B	ⓝ 고속버스(高速bus)	highway bus
A	ⓝ 고양이	cat
C	ⓐ 고요하다	(be) silent

C	d 고작	at the most
B	n 고장	❶ district
		❷ producing center
B	n 고장(故障)	❶ breakdown
		❷ obstacle
C	n 고전(古典)	❶ classics
		❷ old book
C	n 고집(固執)(하)	stubbornness
C	v 고집하다(固執-)[-지파-]	persist
B	n 고추	red pepper
B	n 고추장(-醬)	Korean hot pepper paste
B	n 고춧가루[-추까-]	powdered red pepper
B	v 고치다	❶ repair ❷ correct
B	n 고통(苦痛)	pain
C	a 고통스럽다(苦痛-)[-따]	(be) painful
A	a 고프다	(be) hungry
C	n 고함(高喊)	shout
A	n 고향(故鄕)	hometown
C	n 곡(曲)	tune

C	ⓝ 곡식(穀食)[-씩]	cereals
C	ⓐ 곤란하다(困難-)[골-]	(be) difficult
A	ⓓ 곧	❶ at once
		❷ in another word
C	ⓐ 곧다[-따]	❶ (be) straight
		❷ (be) honest
B	ⓓ 곧바로[-빠-]	❶ straight ❷ frank
C	ⓓ 곧이어[고디-]	one after another
C	ⓓ 곧잘[-짤]	❶ fairly well
		❷ frequently
C	ⓓ 곧장[-짱]	directly
C	ⓝ 골(goal)	❶ goal
		❷ finish line
C	ⓓ 골고루	equally
B	ⓝ 골목	alley
B	ⓝ 골목길[-낄]	alley
C	ⓝ 골짜기	valley
C	ⓝ 골치	head
B	ⓝ 골프(golf)	golf
B	ⓝ 골프장(golf場)	golf-links
B	ⓝ 곰	bear

B	ⓐ 곱다[-따]	❶ (be) pretty
		❷ (be) warm hearted
		❸ (be) sweet <voice>
A	ⓝ 곳[곧]	place
B	ⓝ 곳곳[곧꼳]	on all sides
A	ⓝ 공	ball
B	ⓝ 공간(空間)	space
C	ⓝ 공개(公開)(하)	opening to the public
C	ⓥ 공개하다(公開-)	open to the public
C	ⓝ 공격(攻擊)(하)	❶ criticize ❷ attack
C	ⓥ 공격하다(攻擊-)[-겨카-]	attack
C	ⓝ 공공(公共)	public
C	ⓝ 공군(空軍)	air force
C	ⓝ 공급(供給)(하)	supply
C	ⓝ 공기(空器)	❶ empty vessel ❷ bowl (for meal)
B	ⓝ 공기(空氣)	air
B	ⓝ 공동(共同)	association

B	n 공무원(公務員)	public official
A	n 공부(工夫)(하)	learning
A	v 공부하다(工夫-)	study
B	n 공사(工事)(하)	construction work
C	n 공식(公式)	❶ formality
		❷ formula \<math\>
C	n 공식적(公式的)[-쩍]	official
C	n 공업(工業)	industry
B	n 공연(公演)(하)	public performance
C	v 공연되다(公演-)	be played
C	n 공연장(公演場)	performance hall
C	v 공연하다(公演-)	play (in a drama)
C	d 공연히(空然-)	vainly
A	n 공원(公園)	park
B	n 공장(工場)	factory
C	n 공주(公主)	princess
C	n 공중(空中)	sky
A	n 공중전화(公衆電話)	public phone
B	n 공짜(空-)	free charge
A	n 공책(空册)	notebook

C	n 공통(共通)	commonness
C	v 공통되다(共通-)	be common
C	n 공통적(共通的)	common
C	n 공통점(共通點)[-쩜]	common point
C	n 공포(恐怖)	horror
A	n 공항(空港)	airport
B	n 공항버스(空港bus)	airport bus
C	n 공해(公害)	environmental pollution
A	n 공휴일(公休日)	legal holiday
C	n 과(科)	department \<university\>
A	n 과(課)	❶ department (of company) ❷ lesson or chapter
C	n 과거(科擧)	state examination during the Joseon Dynasty
B	n 과거(過去)	past \<tense\>
B	n 과목(科目)	subject
C	d 과연(果然)	indeed

C n	과외(課外)	① out-of school
		② extra
A n	과일	fruit
A n	과자(菓子)	sweets
B n	과장(課長)	department chief
C n	과정(課程)	course <curriculum>
C n	과정(過程)	process
B n	과제(課題)	① theme
		② homework
B n	과학(科學)	science
B n	과학자(科學者)[-짜]	scientist
B n	과학적(科學的)[-쩍]	scientific
B n	관객(觀客)	spectator
B n	관계(關係)(하)[-게]	① connection
		② concern
C v	관계되다(關係-)[-게-]	have something to do with
C d	관계없이(關係-)[-게업씨]	regardlessly
C n	관계자(關係者)[-게-]	person concerned
B n	관광(觀光)(하)	sightseeing
B n	관광객(觀光客)	tourist

C	n 관광버스(觀光bus)	tourist bus
B	n 관광지(觀光地)	sightseeing place
C	n 관념(觀念)	notion
C	n 관람(觀覽)(하)[괄-]	watching
C	n 관람객(觀覽客)[괄-]	spectator
B	n 관련(關聯)(하)[괄-]	relation
B	v 관련되다(關聯-)[괄-]	be related to
B	v 관련하다(關聯-)[괄-]	relate to
B	n 관리(管理)(하)[괄-]	administration
C	n 관리(官吏)[괄-]	government employee
C	v 관리하다(管理-)[괄-]	administer
C	n 관습(慣習)	convention
B	n 관심(關心)(하)	concern
C	n 관심사(關心事)	matter of concern
C	n 관점(觀點)[-쩜]	viewpoint
C	n 관찰(觀察)(하)	observation
B	v 관찰하다(觀察-)	observe
B	v 관하다(關-)	have something to do with
C	n 광경(光景)	spectacle

B	ⓝ 광고(廣告)(하)	advertisement
C	ⓝ 광장(廣場)	plaza
B	ⓝ 광주(光州)	Gwangju
A	ⓐ 괜찮다[-찬타]	(be) permissible
B	ⓓ 괜히	uselessly
C	ⓝ 괴로움	trouble
C	ⓥ 괴로워하다	be worried
B	ⓐ 괴롭다[-따]	(be) painful
C	ⓥ 괴롭히다[-로피-]	torment
C	ⓐ 굉장하다(宏壯-)	❶(be) magnificent ❷(be) numerous
B	ⓓ 굉장히(宏壯-)	very much
A	ⓝ 교과서(敎科書)	textbook
C	ⓝ 교내(校內)	campus
C	ⓝ 교대(交代)(하)	rotation
B	ⓝ 교류(交流)(하)	❶interchange ❷alternating current
B	ⓝ 교문(校門)	school gate
C	ⓝ 교복(校服)	school uniform
C	ⓝ 교사(敎師)	teacher
A	ⓝ 교수(敎授)	professor

C	n 교시(校時)	class or hour (ex. in the 3rd hour)
C	n 교양(教養)(하)	❶ culture ❷ education
C	n 교외(郊外)	suburbs
B	n 교육(教育)(하)	education
C	n 교육비(教育費)[-삐]	educational expenses
C	n 교육자(教育者)[-짜]	educator
C	n 교장(校長)	principal
C	n 교재(教材)	teaching materials
C	n 교직(教職)	teaching profession
C	n 교체(交替)(하)	replacement
A	n 교통(交通)	traffic
B	n 교통사고(交通事故)	traffic accident
B	n 교포(僑胞)	Korean resident abroad
B	n 교환(交換)(하)	exchange
C	v 교환하다(交換-)	exchange
A	n 교회(教會)	church
C	n 교훈(教訓)	❶ (moral) teaching ❷ lesson

A	ⓤ 구(九)	nine
C	ⓝ 구(區)	gu or ward <administrative district>
A	ⓝ 구경(하)	seeing
B	ⓥ 구경하다	see the sight
A	ⓝ 구두	(men's or ladies') shoes
C	ⓥ 구르다	roll
A	ⓝ 구름	cloud
B	ⓝ 구멍	❶ hole ❷ deficit
C	ⓝ 구별(區別)(하)	distinguishment
C	ⓥ 구별되다(區別-)	be distinguished
C	ⓥ 구별하다(區別-)	distinguish
C	ⓝ 구분(區分)(하)	division
C	ⓥ 구분되다	be classified
C	ⓥ 구분하다(區分-)	classify
C	ⓝ 구석	corner
C	ⓝ 구석구석[-꾸-]	all the corners
C	ⓝ 구성(構成)(하)	❶ construction <sentence, theory>

		❷ plot
C	ⓥ 구성되다(構成-)	organize
C	ⓥ 구성하다(構成-)	organize
C	ⓝ 구속(拘束)(하)	restriction
C	ⓥ 구속되다(拘束-)	be placed under restraint
C	ⓥ 구속하다(拘束-)[-소카-]	restrict
A	ⓤ 구십(九十)	ninety
C	ⓝ 구역(區域)	❶ sphere ❷ zone
A	ⓝ 구월(九月)	September
C	ⓝ 구입(購入)(하)	purchase
C	ⓥ 구입하다[-이파-]	purchase
C	ⓝ 구조(構造)	structure
C	ⓝ 구청(區廳)	gu or ward office <administrative>
B	ⓝ 구체적(具體的)	definite
B	ⓥ 구하다(救-)	rescue
B	ⓥ 구하다(求-)	❶ buy ❷ desire
B	ⓝ 국	broth
B	ⓝ 국가(國家)[-까]	nation
C	ⓝ 국가적(國家的))[-까-]	national

B ⓝ	국기(國旗)[-끼]	national flag
B ⓝ	국내(國內)[궁-]	interior of a country
C ⓝ	국내선(國內線)[궁-]	domestic air service
C ⓝ	국내외(國內外)[궁-]	inside and outside of the country
B ⓝ	국립(國立)[궁닙]	government-established
B ⓝ	국물[궁-]	gravy (of broth)
B ⓝ	국민(國民)[궁-]	a member of a nation
C ⓝ	국민적(國民的)[궁-]	national
C ⓝ	국사(國史)[-싸]	national history
C ⓝ	국산(國産)[-싼]	domestic production
B ⓝ	국수[-쑤]	noodles
B ⓝ	국어(國語)[구거]	Korean language
C ⓝ	국왕(國王)[구광]	king
C ⓝ	국적(國籍)[-쩍]	nationality
B ⓝ	국제(國際)[-쩨]	international
C ⓝ	국제선(國際線)[-쩨-]	international lines
C ⓝ	국제적(國際的)[-쩨-]	international
C ⓝ	국제화(國際化)[-쩨-]	internationalization

C	ⓝ 국회(國會)[구쾨]	National Assembly
B	ⓝ 국회의원(國會議員)[구쾨-]	National Assemblyman
B	ⓝ 군(君)	❶ king ❷ Mr.
B	ⓝ 군(軍)	army
C	ⓝ 군(郡)	gun or county <administrative district>
B	ⓝ 군대(軍隊)	troops
B	ⓝ 군데	place
C	ⓝ 군사(軍事)	military affairs
C	ⓝ 군사(軍士)	soldier
A	ⓝ 군인(軍人)[구닌]	military personnel
C	ⓐ 굳다[-따]	❶ (be) hard ❷ (be) secure
C	ⓥ 굳어지다[구더-]	harden
B	ⓓ 굳이[구지]	❶ firmly ❷ particularly
C	ⓥ 굳히다[구치-]	strengthen
B	ⓐ 굵다[국따]	❶ (be) thick ❷ (be) coarse

		❸ (be) deep \<voice\>
C Ⓥ	굶다[굼따]	starve
B Ⓥ	굽다[-따]	❶ broil
		❷ roast or bake
		❸ burn (bricks)
C Ⓥ	굽히다[구피-]	❶ bend ❷ concede
C Ⓝ	궁극적(窮極的)[-쩍]	ultimate
B Ⓐ	궁금하다	❶ (be) curious
		❷ (be) somewhat hungry
A Ⓝ	권(卷)	❶ volume, book
		❷ the number of book
C Ⓝ	권리(權利)[궐-]	right
C Ⓝ	권위(權威)[궈뉘]	authority
B Ⓝ	권투(拳鬪)	boxing
B Ⓥ	권하다(勸-)	advise
A Ⓝ	귀	❶ ear
		❷ eye of a needle
C Ⓝ	귀가(歸家)(하)	homecoming
C Ⓥ	귀가하다(歸家-)	come home

B	n 귀국(歸國)(하)	return to one's country
B	v 귀국하다[-구카-]	return to one's country
C	n 귀신(鬼神)	❶ghost ❷expert
B	a 귀엽다[-따]	(be) cute
C	a 귀중하다(貴重-)	(be) precious
C	a 귀찮다[-찬타]	(be) annoying
C	a 귀하다(貴-)	❶(be) rare ❷(be) honorable
C	n 귓속[귀쏙]	inner ear
C	n 규모(規模)	scale
C	n 규정(規定)(하)	provision
B	n 규칙(規則)(하)	regulation
B	n 규칙적(規則的)[-쩍]	regular
C	n 균형(均衡)	balance
C	n 귤(橘)	tangerine
A	o 그	the
A	e 그	that
A	r 그	that
C	n 그간(-間)	meanwhile

A	ⓞ 그거	that
A	ⓞ 그것[-걷]	that one
A	ⓞ 그곳[-곧]	that place
C	ⓓ 그나마	❶ even so ❷ especially
A	ⓝ 그날	that day
B	ⓓ 그냥	❶ as it is ❷ throughout
C	ⓞ 그녀(-女)	she
C	ⓞ 그놈	that fellow
B	ⓝ 그늘	❶ shade ❷ gloom
B	ⓝ 그다음	next
B	ⓓ 그다지	❶ not much ❷ to that extent
C	ⓞ 그대	you
B	ⓓ 그대로	intactly
A	ⓝ 그동안	meantime
A	ⓝ 그때	that time
C	ⓓ 그때그때	each time
A	ⓔ 그래	answer of "yes" or "no"

A d	그래서	so, for that reason
A d	그래서	abbr. of so
C n	그래픽(graphic)	graphic
B n	그램(gram)	gram
A d	그러나	but
A d	그러니까	for that reason
C v	그러다	do so, say so
A d	그러면	if that happens
B d	그러므로	therefore
B a	그러하다	(be) so
B r	그런	such
C d	그런대로	passably
A d	그런데	however
C a	그럴듯하다[-뜨타-]	❶(be) passable
		❷(be) seeming
A e	그럼	certainly
A d	그럼	if so
B d	그렇게[-러케]	so
A a	그렇다[-러타]	(be) so
B e	그렇지[-러치]	So it is.
A d	그렇지만[-러치-]	though

B	v 그려지다	be drawn (in one's heart)
C	n 그루	stump
B	n 그룹(group)	group
A	n 그릇[-른]	❶ vessel ❷ capacity
B	d 그리	❶ not very ❷ that ❸ that way
A	d 그리고	and
A	v 그리다	❶ draw ❷ describe ❸ long for
C	d 그리로	there
C	n 그리움	yearning
C	v 그리워하다	miss
C	d 그리하여	so
A	n 그림	picture
B	n 그림자	❶ shadow ❷ trace (of person)
B	a 그립다[-따]	❶ (be) missed ❷ (be) inconvenienced by not

B	d 그만	having ① enough ② right now ③ unavoidably
B	v 그만두다	cut out
B	d 그만큼	to that extent
B	a 그만하다	① (be) about the same ② (be) so-so ③ (be) tolerable
A	o 그분	that gentleman
C	n 그사이	meantime
C	d 그야말로	indeed
C	o 그이	he
C	d 그저	① still or continuously ② aimlessly
C	n 그저께	the day before yesterday
C	n 그전(-前)	former days
C	d 그제서야	at last

C	d 그제야	at last
B	n 그중(-中)	among them
A	o 그쪽	the other side
B	v 그치다	stop <rain, snow or crying>
C	d 그토록	to such an extent
B	n 그해	the year
C	n 극(劇)	drama
C	n 극복(克服)(하)[-뽁]	conquest
C	v 극복하다[-뽀카-]	overcome
C	n 극작가(劇作家)[-짝까-]	playwriter
A	n 극장(劇場)[-짱]	theater
C	d 극히(極-)[그키]	extremely
C	n 근거(根據)(하)	foundation
C	v 근거하다(根據-)	be based (on)
C	n 근교(近郊)	suburbs
B	d 근데	by the way
C	n 근래(近來)[글-]	these days
C	n 근로(勤勞)(하)[글-]	work
B	n 근로자(勤勞者)[글-]	worker
B	n 근무(勤務)(하)	work

B	ⓥ 근무하다(勤務-)	work
C	ⓝ 근본(根本)	essence
C	ⓝ 근본적(根本的)	fundamental
C	ⓝ 근원(根源)[그뭔]	origin
C	ⓝ 근육(筋肉)[그늌]	muscle
A	ⓝ 근처(近處)	vicinity
B	ⓝ 글	❶ a piece of writing
		❷ character
		❸ scholarship
		\<studies\>
B	ⓔ 글쎄	well
B	ⓔ 글쎄요	Let me see.
B	ⓝ 글쓰기	writing
B	ⓝ 글씨	❶ penmanship
		❷ character
		❸ how to write
B	ⓝ 글자(-字)[-짜]	character
C	ⓥ 긁다[극따]	❶ scratch
		❷ scrape up
		❸ offend
C	ⓝ 금	line

B	n 금(金)	gold
C	n 금강산(金剛山)	Mt.Guemgang
C	n 금고(金庫)	safe or strong box
B	n 금년(今年)	this year
C	n 금메달(金medal)	gold medal
B	d 금방(今方)	❶ just now ❷ (just) a moment ago
C	d 금세	in a moment
C	n 금액(金額)[그맥]	amount
B	n 금연(禁煙)[그면]	❶ No smoking ❷ quit smoking
A	n 금요일(金曜日)[그묘일]	Friday
B	n 금지(禁止)(하)	inhibition
C	v 금지되다(禁止-)	be prohibited
B	v 금지하다(禁止-)	prohibit
C	v 금하다(禁-)	prohibit
A	n 급(級)	rank, grade
C	d 급격히(急激-)[-껴키]	rapidly
C	d 급속히(急速-)[-쏘키]	promptly
C	v 급증하다(急增-)[-쯩-]	increase rapidly

B	ⓐ 급하다(急-)[그파-]	❶ (be) urgent
		❷ (be) hasty
C	ⓓ 급히(急-)[그피]	quickly
C	ⓥ 긋다[귿따]	draw
B	ⓝ 긍정적(肯定的)	positive
C	ⓝ 기(旗)	flag
C	ⓝ 기(氣)	❶ breath
		❷ energy
		❸ spirits
B	ⓝ 기간(期間)	period
B	ⓝ 기계(機械)[-게]	machine
C	ⓝ 기관(機關)	❶ machine or engine
		❷ organization or institution
C	ⓝ 기구(器具)	tool
C	ⓝ 기구(機構)	organization
C	ⓝ 기기(器機)	machinery and tools
C	ⓝ 기념(紀念)(하)	commemoration
C	ⓝ 기념일(紀念日)[기녀밀]	anniversary

C n	기념품(紀念品)	souvenir
C v	기념하다(紀念-)	commemorate
C n	기능(技能)	ability
C n	기능(機能)	function
C v	기다	❶ creep
		❷ cringe (to the boss)
A v	기다리다	wait for
B n	기대(期待)(하)	expectation
C v	기대다	lean
C v	기대되다(期待-)	expect
B v	기대하다(期待-)	expect
B n	기도(祈禱)(하)	prayer
C v	기도하다(祈禱-)	pray
C n	기독교(基督敎)[-교]	Christianity
C n	기둥	❶ pillar
		❷ support \<person\>
C n	기록(記錄)(하)	record
C v	기록되다(記錄-)	be recorded
B v	기록하다[-로카-]	record
B v	기르다	❶ raise (pigs)

		❷ build up (strength)
		❸ grow (hair)
		❹ become worse
		<illness>
B	ⓝ 기름	❶ oil ❷ fat
C	ⓐ 기막히다(氣-)[-마키-]	❶ (be) stifle
		❷ (be) stunned
		❸ (be) miserable
		❹ (be) striking
C	ⓝ 기법(技法)[-뻡]	techniques
B	ⓝ 기본(基本)	basis
C	ⓝ 기본적(基本的)	fundamental
A	ⓝ 기분(氣分)	❶ one's heart
		❷ mood
B	ⓥ 기뻐하다	be pleased with
B	ⓐ 기쁘다	(be) happy
B	ⓝ 기쁨	pleasure
B	ⓝ 기사(技士)	engineer
B	ⓝ 기사(記事)	❶ article
		❷ description
C	ⓝ 기성(旣成)	preexisting

		condition
C	n 기성세대(既成世代)	old generation
A	n 기숙사(寄宿舍)[-싸]	dormitory
B	n 기술(技術)	technology
C	n 기술자(技術者)[-짜]	technical expert
C	v 기술하다(記述-)	describe
B	n 기억(記憶)(하)	memory
B	v 기억나다[엉-]	recall
C	v 기억되다(記憶-)	be remembered
B	v 기억하다[-어카-]	remember
C	n 기업(企業)	enterprise
C	n 기업인(企業人)[-어빈]	enterpriser
C	n 기여(寄與)(하)	contribution
C	v 기여하다(寄與-)	contribute
B	n 기온(氣溫)	(atmospheric) temperature
B	n 기운	strength
C	v 기울다	slant
C	v 기울이다[-우리-]	❶ concentrate ❷ drink (liquor)
C	n 기원(起原)	origin

C n	기원전(紀元前)	B.C.
B n	기자(記者)	journalist
C n	기적(奇跡)	miracle
B n	기준(基準)	standard
A n	기차(汽車)	train
B n	기초(基礎)(하)	basis
C n	기초적(基礎的)	basic
C v	기초하다(基礎-)	be based
B n	기침	cough
C n	기타(其他)	and so on
B n	기타(guitar)	guitar
C n	기호(記號)	mark
C n	기혼(旣婚)	married
B n	기회(機會)	opportunity
C n	기획(企劃)(하)	planning
C n	기후(氣候)	climate
C n	긴급(緊急)(하)	emergency
B n	긴장(緊張)(하)	tension
C n	긴장감(緊張感)	suspense
C v	긴장되다(緊張-)	become tense
B v	긴장하다(緊張-)	become tense

A	ⓝ 길	road
B	ⓝ 길가[-까]	roadside
B	ⓝ 길거리[-꺼-]	street
A	ⓐ 길다	(be) long
C	ⓥ 길어지다[기러-]	be lengthened
B	ⓝ 길이[기리]	length
B	ⓝ 김	laver
C	ⓝ 김	❶ vapor ❷ breath
C	ⓝ 김	opportunity
A	ⓝ 김밥[-빱]	rice rolled in dried-laver
A	ⓝ 김치	kimchi
B	ⓝ 김치찌개	kimchi stew
B	ⓝ 김포공항(金浦空港)	Gimpo airport
B	ⓐ 깊다[깁따]	❶ (be) deep ❷ (be) intimate
C	ⓓ 깊숙이[깁쑤기]	deeply
B	ⓓ 깊이[기피]	deeply
B	ⓝ 깊이[기피]	depth
C	ⓥ 까다	❶ peel ❷ hatch
B	ⓝ 까닭[-닥]	reason

B	n 까만색(-色)	black
B	a 까맣다[-마타]	❶(be) black
		❷(be) deep-black
		❸(be) ignorant
C	v 까먹다[-따]	❶peel and eat
		❷go through (a fund)
		❸forget
C	n 까치	magpie
C	n 깍두기[-뚜-]	sliced white-radish kimchi
A	v 깎다[깍따]	❶sharpen ❷shave ❸cut down (the price)
C	a 깔끔하다	(be) sleek and clean
C	v 깔다	❶pave, spread ❷look downward
C	v 깔리다	be paved, be covered
B	d 깜빡	❶with a flash ❷suddenly

B	d 깜짝	all of a sudden
C	n 깡패(-牌)	gangster
B	d 깨끗이[-끄시]	cleanly
A	a 깨끗하다[-끄타-]	(be) clean
C	v 깨끗해지다[-끄태-]	cleanse
B	v 깨다	❶break ❷cancel
B	v 깨다	❶wake up ❷perceive
C	v 깨닫다[-따]	realize
C	n 깨달음[-다름]	awareness
C	v 깨뜨리다	❶break ❷frustrate (one's plan)
C	n 깨소금	powdered sesame mixed with salt
C	v 깨어나다	recover consciousness
C	v 깨어지다	be broken
C	v 깨우다	wake up
B	v 깨지다	❶be broken ❷be shipwrecked
B	v 꺼내다	❶pull out

		❷ start (talking)
B	Ⓥ 꺼지다	blow out
C	Ⓥ 꺾다[꺽따]	❶ break off
		❷ turn to
B	Ⓝ 껌(gum)	(chewing) gum
B	Ⓝ 껍질[-찔]	peel
C	Ⓝ 꼬리	tag
C	Ⓝ 꼬마	kid
A	Ⓓ 꼭	❶ sure ❷ just
		❸ completely
C	Ⓓ 꼭	❶ always
		❷ firmly
B	Ⓝ 꼭대기[-때-]	summit
C	Ⓝ 꼴	shape
C	Ⓐ 꼼꼼하다	(be) very careful
C	Ⓓ 꼼짝	budging slightly
C	Ⓥ 꼽히다[꼬피-]	be counted (on one's fingers)
C	Ⓥ 꽂다[꼳따]	❶ fix
		❷ put (a bar) across
A	Ⓝ 꽃[꼳]	flower

C	ⓝ 꽃씨[꼳-]	flower seed
B	ⓝ 꽃잎[꼰닙]	petal
C	ⓓ 꽉	❶ closely ❷ fast ❸ entirely
B	ⓓ 꽤	quite
B	ⓥ 꾸다	dream
C	ⓥ 꾸다	borrow
C	ⓥ 꾸리다	❶ pack up ❷ decorate ❸ manage (household, work)
B	ⓥ 꾸미다	❶ decorate ❷ fabricate (an alibi) ❸ form (organization)
C	ⓐ 꾸준하다	(be) steady
B	ⓓ 꾸준히	steadily
C	ⓝ 꾸중(하)	scolding
B	ⓝ 꿀	honey
A	ⓝ 꿈	dream
B	ⓥ 꿈꾸다	❶ have a dream

		❷ dream of
B	ⓝ 꿈속[-쏙]	in one's dream
A	ⓥ 끄다	❶ put out (fire)
		❷ turn off (TV)
B	ⓥ 끄덕이다[-더기-]	nod
C	ⓝ 끈	string
C	ⓥ 끊기다[끈키-]	be cut
B	ⓥ 끊다[끈타]	❶ cut ❷ buy
		❸ sever (relations)
		❹ give up
B	ⓥ 끊어지다[끄너-]	be cut
C	ⓐ 끊임없다[끄니멉따]	(be) continuous
C	ⓓ 끊임없이[끄니멉씨]	constantly
B	ⓥ 끌다	❶ pull ❷ delay
		❸ attract
C	ⓥ 끌리다	❶ be attracted
		❷ be drawn
C	ⓥ 끌어당기다[끄러-]	tug
B	ⓥ 끓다[끌타]	❶ boil ❷ flock
		❸ burn (with anger)
B	ⓥ 끓이다[끄리-]	boil

A ⓝ끝[끋]	❶end ❷edge
A ⓥ끝나다[끈-]	❶end ❷be over
B ⓓ끝내[끈-]	to the last
A ⓥ끝내다[끈-]	end
C ⓐ끝없다[끄덥-]	(be) endless
C ⓓ끝없이[끄덥씨]	endlessly
C ⓝ끼	meal
B ⓥ끼다	❶be foggy ❷take part in
B ⓥ끼다	❶overlap ❷wear
C ⓥ끼어들다	intrude into
C ⓥ끼우다	insert

ㄴ

A	ⓞ 나	I
A	ⓢ 나가다	…ing
A	ⓥ 나가다	❶ get out
		❷ step (walk)
		❸ proceed
B	ⓥ 나누다	❶ divide
		❷ share
		❸ converse
C	ⓥ 나누어지다	be divided
C	ⓥ 나뉘다	be divided
B	ⓢ 나다	❶ continue
		❷ be over
A	ⓥ 나다	❶ be born
		❷ grow ❸ happen
		❹ come out (smell)
C	ⓝ 나들이(하)[-드리]	❶ outing
		❷ going in and out
A	ⓝ 나라	nation
C	ⓓ 나란히	evenly

106

C	v 나르다	carry
C	n 나름	depending on
B	n 나머지	❶ surplus
		❷ remainder
A	n 나무	❶ tree
		❷ timber
B	n 나물	❶ wild greens
		❷ seasoned vegetables
B	n 나뭇가지[-무까-]	branch
B	n 나뭇잎[-문닙-]	leaf
B	n 나비	butterfly
B	v 나빠지다	get worse
A	a 나쁘다	(be) bad
B	v 나서다	❶ step forward
		❷ turn up
C	v 나아가다	❶ advance
		❷ get better
C	v 나아지다	get better
A	v 나오다	❶ come out
		❷ come

A ⓝ 나이	age
A ⓝ 나중	❶ latter part
	❷ finale
C ⓝ 나침반(羅針盤)	compass
B ⓥ 나타나다	❶ appear
	❷ come into view
B ⓥ 나타내다	express
B ⓝ 나흘	❶ four days
	❷ the fourth day of the month
B ⓝ 낙엽(落葉)[나겹]	fallen leaves
B ⓝ 낚시[낙씨]	❶ fishing
	❷ (fish) hook
C ⓝ 낚시꾼[낙씨-]	fisherman
C ⓝ 낚싯대[낙씨때]	fishing rod
C ⓝ 난리(亂離)[날-]	disturbance
C ⓝ 난방(暖房)	❶ heating
	❷ heated room
A ⓝ 날	❶ day ❷ weather
	❸ date
B ⓝ 날개	wing

A	v 날다	❶ fly ❷ run away ❸ evaporate
C	v 날리다	❶ let fly ❷ scamp (one's work) ❸ lose
A	n 날씨	weather
B	v 날아가다[나라-]	❶ fly away ❷ be gone ❸ evaporate
C	v 날아다니다[나라-]	fly around
B	v 날아오다[나라-]	fly over
A	n 날짜	❶ day ❷ date
C	a 날카롭다[-따]	❶ (be) sharp ❷ (be) cutting ❸ (be) quick-witted
B	a 낡다[낙따]	(be) old-fashioned
C	n 남	❶ others ❷ unrelated person

B	ⓝ 남(南)	south
B	ⓝ 남(男)	man
B	ⓥ 남기다	leave behind
A	ⓝ 남녀(男女)	man and woman
B	ⓥ 남다[-따]	remain
A	ⓝ 남대문(南大門)	Namdaemun
A	ⓝ 남대문시장(南大門市場)	Namdaemun market
A	ⓝ 남동생(男同生)	one's little brother
B	ⓝ 남매(男妹)	brother and sister
C	ⓝ 남미(南美)	South America
C	ⓝ 남부(南部)	southern part
C	ⓝ 남북(南北)	north and south
B	ⓝ 남산(南山)	the Namsan
B	ⓝ 남성(男性)	male
A	ⓝ 남자(男子)	man
A	ⓝ 남쪽(南-)	south
A	ⓝ 남편(男便)	husband
A	ⓝ 남학생(男學生)[-쌩]	boy student
C	ⓥ 납득하다(納得-)[-뜨카-]	understand

B	ⓥ 낫다[낟따]	recover from an illness
B	ⓐ 낫다[낟따]	(be) superior
C	ⓝ 낭비(浪費)(하)	waste
A	ⓝ 낮[낟]	daytime
A	ⓐ 낮다[낟따]	(be) low
C	ⓥ 낮아지다[나자-]	get lower
C	ⓥ 낮추다[낟-]	lower
B	ⓐ 낯설다[낟썰-]	(be) unfamiliar
C	ⓝ 낱말[난-]	word
B	ⓥ 낳다[나타]	give birth to
C	ⓝ 내	within
C	ⓝ 내과(內科)[-꽈]	internal medicine
B	ⓓ 내내	❶from beginning to end ❷forever
A	ⓝ 내년(來年)	next year
B	ⓥ 내놓다[-노타]	❶take out ❷expose
A	ⓢ 내다	do all the way (to the very end)
A	ⓥ 내다	❶take out

		❷ divide
		❸ share (time)
C	v 내다보다	❶ look out
		❷ foresee
C	n 내달(來-)	next month
A	v 내려가다	❶ go down
		❷ drop
B	v 내려놓다[-노타]	bring down
B	v 내려다보다	look down
A	v 내려오다	❶ come down
		❷ (above) come from
C	v 내려지다	be lowered
A	v 내리다	❶ descend
		❷ reduce
B	v 내밀다	push out
C	v 내버리다	throw away
C	v 내보내다	❶ let out
		❷ lay off
C	n 내부(內部)	inner part
C	v 내쉬다	❶ breathe out

		❷ sigh
C	ⓝ 내외(內外)(하)	avoidance of the opposite sex
C	ⓝ 내외(內外)	❶ inside and outside
		❷ husband and wife
B	ⓝ 내용(內容)	contents
C	ⓝ 내용물(內容物)	contents<goods>
A	ⓝⓓ 내일(來日)	tomorrow
C	ⓝ 내적(內的)[-쩍]	internal
C	ⓥ 내주다	❶ grant
		❷ resign
B	ⓓ 내지(乃至)	❶ from…to
		❷ and
C	ⓝ 내후년(來後年)	year after next
B	ⓝ 냄비	saucepan
B	ⓝ 냄새	smell
C	ⓝ 냇물[낸-]	stream
C	ⓝ 냉동(冷凍)(하)	refrigeration
A	ⓝ 냉면(冷麵)	cold noodles
C	ⓝ 냉방(冷房)	air-condition
A	ⓝ 냉장고(冷藏庫)	refrigerator

A ⓞ 너	you
B ⓝ 너머	beyond
A ⓓ 너무	too
B ⓓ 너무나	too
B ⓞ 너희[-히]	you all
C ⓡ 넉	four
C ⓐ 넉넉하다[넝너카-]	(be) enough
C ⓓ 널리	❶ widely
	❷ generously
A ⓐ 넓다[널따]	❶ (be) wide
	❷ (be) extensive
B ⓥ 넓어지다[널버-]	become wider
B ⓥ 넓히다[널피-]	❶ widen
	❷ expand
C ⓥ 넘겨주다	transfer
C ⓥ 넘기다	❶ throw down
	❷ hand over
	❸ keep over
B ⓥ 넘다[-따]	❶ exceed
	❷ conquer
B ⓥ 넘어가다[너머-]	❶ fall down ❷ cross

		❸ fall into (one's hands)
C	ⓥ 넘어뜨리다[너머-]	throw down
B	ⓥ 넘어서다[너머-]	pass over
C	ⓥ 넘어오다[너머-]	come over
B	ⓥ 넘어지다[너머-]	❶ be ruined
		❷ fall over
B	ⓥ 넘치다	overflow
A	ⓥ 넣다[너타]	❶ put ❷ inset
A	ⓡ 네	four
A	ⓔ 네	yes
B	ⓝ 네거리	crossroads
A	ⓝ 넥타이(necktie)	necktie
A	ⓤ 넷[넫]	four
A	ⓡ 넷째[넫-]	fourth
B	ⓝ 녀석	guy
A	ⓝ 년(年)	year
B	ⓝ 년대(年代)	historical date
B	ⓝ 년도(年度)	year
C	ⓝ 년생(年生)	yearly
C	ⓝ 노동(勞動)(하)	work

B	n 노동자(勞動者)	worker
A	n 노란색(-色)	yellow
B	a 노랗다[-라타]	(be) yellow
A	n 노래(하)	song
B	n 노래방(-房)	singing room furnished with a karaoke
A	v 노래하다	sing (a song)
B	n 노랫소리[-래쏘-]	singing voice
B	n 노력(努力)(하)	effort
B	v 노력하다(努力-)[-려카-]	strive
C	n 노선(路線)	route
B	n 노인(老人)	old person
A	n 노트(note)(하)	note
C	v 녹다[-따]	❶ dissolve ❷ melt
B	n 녹색(綠色)[-쌕]	green
B	n 녹음(錄音)(하)[노금]	sound recording
B	v 녹음하다(錄音-)[노금-]	phonograph
C	v 녹이다[노기-]	melt
B	n 녹차(綠茶)	green tea

C	n 녹화(錄畵)(하)[노콰]	video recording
C	n 논	rice field
C	n 논리(論理)[놀-]	logic
C	n 논리적(論理的)[놀-]	logical
B	n 논문(論文)	treatise
B	v 논의하다(論議-)[노니-]	discuss
C	n 논쟁(論爭)(하)	argument
C	v 논하다(論-)	comment on
A	v 놀다	❶ play
		❷ be idle (one's time)
		❸ stop
		❹ be doing nothing
A	v 놀라다	❶ be surprised
		❷ be frightened
		❸ be astonished
B	a 놀랍다[-따]	(be) surprising
C	v 놀리다	tease
B	n 놀이(하)[노리]	game
B	n 놀이터[노리-]	playground
C	n 놈	guy
B	n 농구(籠球)	basketball

B	n 농담(弄談)(하)	joke
C	n 농민(農民)	farmer
C	n 농부(農夫)	peasant
B	n 농사(農事)	farming
C	n 농사일(農事-)	farmwork
C	v 농사짓다(農事-)[-짇따]	farm
C	n 농산물(農産物)	agricultural products
B	n 농업(農業)	agriculture
C	n 농장(農場)	farm
B	n 농촌(農村)	farm village
A	a 높다[놉따]	(be) high
B	v 높아지다[노파-]	get higher
B	n 높이[노피]	height
B	d 높이[노피]	highly
B	v 높이다[노피-]	heighten
A	s 놓다[노타]	maintain
A	v 놓다[노타]	❶ lay ❷ set
C	v 놓아두다[노-]	❶ untouched \<things\>

118

		❷ let alone
B	ⓥ 놓이다[노-]	be put
B	ⓥ 놓치다[노-]	❶ lose
		❷ miss (opportunity)
C	ⓥ 놔두다	❶ untouched \<things\>
		❷ let alone
C	ⓝ 뇌(腦)	❶ brain ❷ head
A	ⓞ 누구	who
A	ⓝ 누나	a boy's elder sister
B	ⓥ 누르다	❶ press ❷ suppress
		❸ overpower
		❹ weigh down
A	ⓝ 눈	eye
A	ⓝ 눈	snow
C	ⓝ 눈가[-까]	eye rims
C	ⓥ 눈감다[-따]	❶ die
		❷ overlook
C	ⓝ 눈길[-낄]	line of sight
C	ⓝ 눈동자(-瞳子)[-똥-]	pupil of the eye
C	ⓥ 눈뜨다	❶ open eyes

	❷wake up
A ⓝ 눈물	tear
C ⓝ 눈병(-病)[-뼝]	eye disease
C ⓐ 눈부시다	❶(be) dazzling
	❷(be) brilliant
B ⓝ 눈빛[-삗]	glitter of one's eyes
B ⓝ 눈썹	eyebrows
B ⓝ 눈앞[누납]	before one's eye
B ⓥ 눕다[-따]	❶lie down
	❷lie sick in bed
A ⓝ 뉴스(news)	news (of TV or radio)
B ⓝ 뉴욕(New York)	New York State or City
B ⓥ 느껴지다	be felt
B ⓥ 느끼다	feel
B ⓝ 느낌	feeling
B ⓐ 느리다	❶(be) slow
	❷(be) loose <in weave>
C ⓝ 늑대[-때]	wolf

B	d	늘	always
B	v	늘다	① increase
			② improve
B	v	늘리다	increase
B	v	늘어나다[느러-]	lengthen
C	v	늘어놓다[느러노타]	① scatter about
			② place in a row
			③ enumerate
C	v	늘어서다[느러-]	stand in a line
C	v	늘어지다[느러-]	① be lengthened
			② droop
			③ languish
			④ live comfortably
B	v	늙다[늑따]	get old
C	n	능동적	active
B	n	능력[-녁]	ability
C	n	늦가을[늗까-]	late autumn
A	a	늦다[늗따]	① (be) late
			② (be) loose
A	v	늦다[늗따]	be late
C	v	늦어지다[느저-]	be late

ㄷ

A	d 다	everything
A	n 다	all
B	v 다가가다	approach
C	v 다가서다	go near
B	v 다가오다	come up to
B	v 다녀가다	drop in
A	v 다녀오다	get back
A	v 다니다	❶ go to and from
		❷ attend
C	v 다듬다[-따]	❶ refine (writings)
		❷ pave
		❸ trim
C	v 다루다	❶ handle
		❷ manage
		❸ conduct
A	a 다르다	❶ (be) different
		❷ (be) unusual
A	r 다른	other
C	a 다름없다[-르멉따]	(be) similar

A	ⓝ 다리	leg
A	ⓝ 다리	bridge
C	ⓓ 다만	only
C	ⓝ 다방(茶房)	teahouse
A	ⓤ 다섯[-섣]	five
A	ⓡ 다섯째[-섣-]	fifth
C	ⓓ 다소(多少)	more or less
B	ⓝ 다수(多數)	large number
A	ⓓ 다시	again
C	ⓝ 다양성(多樣性)[-썽]	diversity
B	ⓐ 다양하다(多樣-)	(be) various
C	ⓥ 다양해지다(多樣-)	diversify
A	ⓝ 다음	next
B	ⓝ 다이어트(diet)(하)	dietary treatment
C	ⓐ 다정하다(多情-)	❶(be) tender ❷(be) kind-hearted
C	ⓥ 다지다	❶harden ❷determine
C	ⓥ 다짐하다	❶pledge ❷warn
B	ⓥ 다치다	❶injure

		❷ hurt ❸ harm
C	ⓥ 다투다	❶ quarrel
		❷ contend (for a prize)
C	ⓝ 다툼(하)	quarrel
B	ⓥ 다하다	❶ finish
		❷ use up
C	ⓝ 다행(多幸)	good fortune
B	ⓓ 다행히(多幸-)	fortunately
C	ⓥ 닥치다	impend
A	ⓥ 닦다[닥따]	❶ polish
		❷ brush (teeth)
		❸ prepare the ground
B	ⓡ 단(單)	only (one)
C	ⓝ 단(段)	❶ paragraph
		❷ step ❸ grade
C	ⓝ 단계(段階)[-계]	step
C	ⓝ 단골	patronage
C	ⓐ 단단하다	❶ (be) solid
		❷ (be) tight

		❸(be) extraordinary
C	ⓝ 단독(單獨)	singleness
B	ⓝ 단맛[-맏]	sweetness
C	ⓝ 단순(單純)(하)	simplicity
B	ⓐ 단순하다(單純-)	(be) simple
B	ⓓ 단순히(單純-)	simply
A	ⓝ 단어(單語)[다너]	vocabulary
C	ⓝ 단위(單位)[다뉘]	unit
B	ⓝ 단점(短點)[-쩜]	weak point
B	ⓓ 단지(但只)	only
B	ⓝ 단지(團地)	housing complex
B	ⓝ 단체(團體)	group
C	ⓝ 단추	❶button
		❷push button
C	ⓝ 단편(短篇)	a short story
C	ⓝ 단풍(丹楓)	❶maple
		❷red leaf
A	ⓥ 닫다[-따]	close
B	ⓥ 닫히다[다치-]	be closed
A	ⓝ 달	moon

A	ⓝ 달	month
B	ⓥ 달걀	egg
B	ⓥ 달다	fasten
B	ⓥ 달다	❶ glow ❷ feverish
C	ⓥ 달다	annotate
A	ⓐ 달다	❶ (be) sweet ❷ (be) appetitive
B	ⓥ 달라지다	change
C	ⓥ 달래다	❶ calm (down) ❷ coax
A	ⓝ 달러(dollar)	dollar
B	ⓥ 달려가다	run
C	ⓥ 달려들다	go at
B	ⓥ 달려오다	come running
A	ⓝ 달력(-曆)	calendar
C	ⓓ 달리	especially
C	ⓝ 달리기(하)	run
B	ⓥ 달리다	rush
B	ⓥ 달리다	hang
C	ⓥ 달리하다	❶ differ ❷ discriminate

B	n 달빛[-삗]	moonlight
B	v 달아나다[다라-]	❶ scud
		❷ escape
		❸ lose <appetite>
A	n 닭[닥]	chickens
A	n 닭고기[닥꼬-]	chicken
B	v 닮다[담따]	resemble
C	n 담	wall
B	v 담그다	❶ soak ❷ pickle
		❸ ferment
B	v 담기다	❶ be put in
		❷ be included in
B	v 담다[담따]	❶ put into
		❷ include
C	n 담당(擔當)(하)	undertaking
C	n 담당자(擔當者)	person in charge
B	v 담당하다(擔當-)	be in charge of
A	n 담배	❶ tobacco plant
		❷ cigarette
B	n 담요[-뇨]	blanket
B	n 담임(擔任)(하)[다밈]	charge

C	ⓝ 답	answer
B	ⓐ 답답하다[-따파-]	❶ be stifled ❷ have difficulty in breathing ❸ be anxious
C	ⓝ 답변(答辯)(하)[-뼌]	❶ reply ❷ excuse
B	ⓝ 답장(答狀)(하)[-짱]	answer
B	ⓥ 답하다(答-)[다파-]	answer
B	ⓝ 닷새[닫쌔]	❶ five days ❷ the fifth day of the month
B	ⓝ 당근	carrot
B	ⓥ 당기다	❶ be attracted ❷ pull ❸ advance
C	ⓐ 당당하다(堂堂-)	❶ (be) fair ❷ (be) grand
C	ⓓ 당분간(當分間)	for some time
C	ⓝ 당시(當時)	at that time
B	ⓞ 당신(當身)	you
B	ⓐ 당연하다(當然-)	(be) right

B	d 당연히(當然-)	rightly
B	n 당장(當場)	on the spot
C	v 당하다(當-)	❶ undergo
		❷ be cheated
B	v 당황하다(唐慌-)	be confused
B	v 닿다[다타]	❶ touch
		❷ arrive
		❸ get in touch
C	n 대	stem
C	n 대	bamboo
C	n 대(代)	family line
B	n 대(對)	versus
B	n 대(臺)	level
C	n 대가(代價)[-까]	❶ price ❷ cost
C	d 대강(大綱)	approximately
C	d 대개(大槪)	mostly
C	n 대개(大槪)	❶ outline
		❷ most
B	n 대구(大邱)	Daegu
C	n 대규모(大規模)	large scale
C	n 대기(大氣)	❶ atmosphere

			❷air
B	n	대기업(大企業)	large enterprise
C	v	대기하다(待機-)	stand by
C	n	대낮[-낟]	broad daylight
C	v	대다	❶touch ❷draw (water) ❸furnish
C	n	대다수(大多數)	large majority
B	a	대단하다	(be) considerable
B	d	대단히	immensely
A	n	대답(對答)(하)	answer
A	v	대답하다(對答-)[-다파-]	answer
B	n	대도시(大都市)	big city
C	n	대략(大略)	❶great strategy ❷outline
C	n	대량(大量)	large quantity
C	n	대로	according to
C	n	대륙(大陸)	continent
B	n	대문(大門)	gate
B	n	대부분(大部分)	most
C	n	대비(對備)(하)	provision

C	v 대비하다(對備-)	prepare
C	n 대사(大使)	ambassador
C	n 대사(臺詞)	one's lines
A	n 대사관(大使館)	embassy
C	n 대상자(對象者)	case <person>
B	n 대신(代身)(하)	replacement
C	v 대신하다(代身-)	be substitute
C	r 대여섯[-섣]	about five or six
C	n 대응(對應)(하)	❶countermeasure ❷correspondence
C	v 대응하다(對應-)	❶confront ❷correspond ❸deal with
C	n 대입(大入)	university entrance examination
B	n 대전(大田)	Daejeon
C	n 대접(待接)(하)	treatment
C	v 대접하다(待接-)[-저파-]	serve
B	n 대중(大衆)	masses
B	n 대중교통(大衆交通)	mass transporta-

		tion
B	n 대중문화(大衆文化)	popular culture
C	n 대중적(大衆的)	popular
C	n 대책(對策)	measure
C	v 대처하다(對處-)	cope with
C	d 대체(大體)	generally
C	d 대체로(大體-)	generally
C	n 대출(貸出)(하)	loan
C	d 대충	almost
B	n 대통령(大統領)[-녕]	president
B	n 대표(代表)(하)	representation
B	n 대표적(代表的)	representative
C	v 대표하다(代表-)	represent
B	v 대하다(對-)	❶face ❷treat ❸resist
A	n 대학(大學)	college
A	n 대학교(大學校)[-꾜]	university
B	n 대학교수(大學敎授)[-꾜-]	university professor
C	n 대학로(大學路)[-항노]	Daehangno
A	n 대학생(大學生)[-쌩]	university student

B	n 대학원(大學院)[-하권]	graduate school
B	n 대한민국(大韓民國)	the Republic of Korea
C	n 대합실(待合室)[-씰]	waiting room <station>
C	n 대형(大型)	large size
A	n 대화(對話)(하)	conversation
B	v 대화하다(對話-)	talk with
B	n 대회(大會)	tournament
A	n 댁(宅)	his esteemed house
C	n 댐(dam)	dam (for water-storage)
A	d 더	❶ even ❷ again
B	d 더구나	in addition
C	d 더더욱	more and more
C	v 더러워지다	get dirty
B	a 더럽다[-따]	❶ (be) dirty ❷ (be) unchaste ❸ (be) ill-tempered

C	ⓥ 더불다	do together
C	ⓓ 더욱	more
C	ⓓ 더욱더[-떠]	more and more
C	ⓓ 더욱이[-우기]	furthermore
B	ⓝ 더위	❶ hot weather
		❷ sunstroke
B	ⓥ 더하다	add
C	ⓝ 덕(德)	❶ virtue
		❷ assistance
B	ⓝ 덕분(德分)[-뿐]	indebtedness
B	ⓝ 덕수궁(德壽宮)[-쑤-]	Deoksugung
B	ⓥ 던지다	❶ throw
		❷ vote
B	ⓓ 덜	less
C	ⓥ 덜다	❶ subtract
		❷ lighten
A	ⓐ 덥다[덥따]	(be) hot
C	ⓥ 덧붙이다[덛뿌치-]	❶ fix
		❷ add something extra
C	ⓝ 덩어리	lump

B ⓥ 덮다[덥따]	❶ cover ❷ hide
C ⓥ 덮이다[더피-]	be covered
B ⓝ 데	place
B ⓥ 데려가다	take (person) along
B ⓥ 데려오다	bring (person) along
B ⓥ 데리다	get accompanied
C ⓥ 데우다	heat
C ⓝ 데이트(date)(하)	date (with other sex)
C ⓝ 도(度)	❶ degree (temperature unit) ❷ (lean) degree
C ⓝ 도(道)	do, province <administrative district>
C ⓝ 도(道)	❶ morality ❷ skill
B ⓝ 도구(道具)	utensil
C ⓥ 도달하다(到達-)	reach

C	d 도대체(都大體)	on earth
C	n 도덕(道德)	morality
B	n 도둑	thief
B	d 도로	back
B	n 도로(道路)	road
C	d 도리어	on the contrary
C	n 도마	chopping board
C	n 도망(逃亡)(하)	escape
B	v 도망가다(逃亡-)	run away
C	v 도망치다(逃亡-)	run away
A	n 도서관(圖書館)	library
A	n 도시(都市)	city
B	n 도시락	lunch box
C	n 도심(都心)	downtown
A	v 도와주다	help
B	n 도움	help
C	n 도움말	help file
C	n 도입(導入)(하)	introduction
B	n 도자기(陶瓷器)	chinaware
C	n 도장(圖章)	stamp
C	d 도저히(到底-)	utterly

C	n 도전(挑戰)(하)	challenge
B	n 도중(途中)	❶halfway
		❷middle
A	n 도착(到着)(하)	arrival
A	v 도착하다(到着-)[-차카-]	arrive
B	n 도쿄(東京)	Tokyo
C	n 독감(毒感)[-깜]	influenza
C	n 독립(獨立)(하)[동닙]	independence
C	v 독립하다(獨立-)[동니파-]	become independent
B	n 독서(讀書)(하)[-써]	reading (books)
A	n 독일(獨逸)[도길]	Germany
B	n 독일어(獨逸語)[도기러]	German language
C	n 독창적(獨創的)	original
C	a 독특하다(獨特-)[-트카-]	(be) unique
C	a 독하다(毒-)[도카-]	❶(be) severe
		❷(be) poisonous
		❸(be) vicious
A	n 돈	money
B	n 돌	stone
B	v 돌다	❶revolve

		❷ circulate
		❸ take effect
B	v 돌려주다	return
B	v 돌리다	❶ pass the crisis
		❷ change (one's mind)
		❸ turn
C	n 돌멩이	a piece of stone
B	v 돌보다	take care of
A	v 돌아가다[도라-]	go back
C	v 돌아다니다[도라-]	wander
B	v 돌아보다[도라-]	❶ look back
		❷ visit
B	v 돌아서다[도라-]	❶ turn against
		❷ get better (illness)
A	v 돌아오다[도라-]	❶ return
		❷ come around \<turn\>
		❸ recover
A	v 돕다[-따]	❶ help

		❷ promote
C	ⓝ 동(同)	the same
C	ⓝ 동(棟)	the number of building
C	ⓝ 동그라미	circle
C	ⓐ 동그랗다[-라타]	(be) round
B	ⓝ 동기(動機)	motive
C	ⓝ 동기(同期)	❶ same period
		❷ same class
B	ⓝ 동네(洞-)	village
B	ⓝ 동대문(東大門)	Dongdaemun
B	ⓝ 동대문시장(東大門市場)	Dongdaemun market
C	ⓝ 동료(同僚)[-뇨]	colleague
A	ⓝ 동물(動物)	animal
B	ⓝ 동물원(動物園)[-무뤈]	zoo
C	ⓝ 동부(東部)	eastern part
A	ⓝ 동생(同生)	younger brother(sister)
C	ⓝ 동서(東西)	the east and the west

C	ⓝ 동서남북(東西南北)	cardinal points
B	ⓝ 동시(同時)	same period
B	ⓝ 동아리	club (with the same purpose)
A	ⓝ 동안	period
B	ⓝ 동양(東洋)	the Orient
C	ⓝ 동양인(東洋人)	an Oriental
C	ⓝ 동의(同意)(하)[-이]	agreement
C	ⓥ 동의하다(同意-)[-이-]	consent
C	ⓐ 동일하다(同一--)	(be) identical
C	ⓝ 동작(動作)(하)	movements
B	ⓝ 동전(銅錢)	copper coin
A	ⓝ 동쪽(東-)	east
B	ⓝ 동창(同窓)	schoolmate
C	ⓝ 동포(同胞)	one's countrymen
C	ⓝ 동행(同行)(하)	❶ going together ❷ fellow travelers
B	ⓝ 동화(童話)	children's story
C	ⓝ 동화책(童話冊)	collection of fairy tales
A	ⓝ 돼지	pig

A	ⓝ 돼지고기	pork
B	ⓓ 되게	very
A	ⓥ 되다	❶ become ❷ reach (time) ❸ be ok
C	ⓥ 되돌리다	restore
C	ⓥ 되돌아가다[-도라-]	turn back
C	ⓥ 되돌아보다[-도라-]	look back on
C	ⓥ 되돌아오다[-도라-]	come back
C	ⓥ 되살리다	❶ raise from the death ❷ recall one's memories
C	ⓥ 되찾다[-찬따]	get back
C	ⓥ 되풀이되다[-푸리-]	be repeated
C	ⓥ 되풀이하다[-푸리-]	repeat
B	ⓝ 된장(-醬)	soybean paste
B	ⓝ 된장찌개	bean-paste pot stew
A	ⓡ 두	two
B	ⓐ 두껍다[-따]	(be) thick

C	ⓝ 두께	thickness
C	ⓝ 두뇌(頭腦)	brains
B	ⓢ 두다	keeping of motion, effect
B	ⓥ 두다	❶ place ❷ leave (behind)
C	ⓐ 두드러지다	(be) remarkable
B	ⓥ 두드리다	beat
C	ⓝ 두려움	fear
C	ⓥ 두려워하다	be afraid of
C	ⓐ 두렵다[-따]	❶ (be) scared ❷ (be) awed
C	ⓥ 두르다	❶ wheel ❷ revolve ❸ surround (clothes)
C	ⓥ 두리번거리다	stare about
B	ⓝ 두부(豆腐)	bean curd
B	ⓡ 두세	two or three
C	ⓡ 두어	about two
B	ⓝ 두통(頭痛)	headache

A	ⓤ 둘	two
B	ⓥ 둘러보다	look around
C	ⓥ 둘러싸다	❶ enclose
		❷ siege
		❸ surround
C	ⓥ 둘러싸이다	be surrounded
A	ⓡ 둘째	second
B	ⓐ 둥글다	(be) round
C	ⓝ 둥지	nest
A	ⓝ 뒤	❶ back
		❷ future
		❸ following
C	ⓐ 뒤늦다[-늗따]	(be) delayed
C	ⓥ 뒤따르다	follow
C	ⓥ 뒤지다	look for
B	ⓥ 뒤집다[-따]	❶ turn over
		❷ reverse
		❸ overthrow
B	ⓝ 뒤쪽	backside
C	ⓝ 뒤편(-便)	backside
C	ⓝ 뒷골목[뒤꼴-]	back street

C	ⓝ 뒷모습[뒫-]	figure from behind
C	ⓝ 뒷문(-門)[뒫-]	back door
B	ⓝ 뒷산(-山)[뒤싼]	mountain at the back
C	ⓓ 드디어	finally
B	ⓝ 드라마(drama)	❶drama (TV or radio) ❷playbook
C	ⓥ 드러나다	❶show ❷disclose ❸become known
A	ⓢ 드리다	honorific of give
A	ⓥ 드리다	honorific of give
C	ⓐ 드물다	❶(be) few ❷(be) rare ❸(be) sparce
A	ⓥ 듣다[-따]	❶hear ❷accept ❸take effect <medicine>
B	ⓝ 들	field

A	Ⓥ 들다	❶ enter
		❷ move in
		❸ check in(hotel)
A	Ⓥ 들다	❶ hold ❷ carry
B	Ⓥ 들다	❶ eat
		❷ cut (well)
B	Ⓥ 들려오다	come into hearing
B	Ⓥ 들려주다	tell
B	Ⓥ 들르다	drop by
B	Ⓥ 들리다	be heard
A	Ⓥ 들어가다[드러-]	❶ enter
		❷ attend
		❸ be inserted
B	Ⓥ 들어서다[드러-]	❶ enter ❷ occupy
A	Ⓥ 들어오다[드러-]	❶ enter
		❷ take part in
		❸ come into view
C	Ⓥ 들어주다[드러-]	grant
C	Ⓥ 들여놓다[드려노타]	❶ take in
		❷ set foot (in)
B	Ⓥ 들여다보다[드려-]	look into

C	ⓥ 들이다[드리-]	dye
C	ⓥ 들이마시다[드리-]	breathe in
C	ⓥ 들이켜다[드리-]	drink down
C	ⓝ 듯[듣]	seem
C	ⓢ 듯싶다[듣씹따]	wonder
B	ⓝ 듯이[드시]	as if
C	ⓢ 듯하다[드타-]	same as
B	ⓝ 등	one's back
B	ⓝ 등(等)	grade
B	ⓝ 등(等)	and so on
C	ⓝ 등등(等等)	etc.
B	ⓝ 등록(登錄)(하)[-녹]	registration
B	ⓝ 등록금(登錄金)[-녹끔]	registration fee
C	ⓝ 등록증(登錄證)[-녹쯩]	certificate of inscription
C	ⓥ 등록하다(登錄-)[-노카-]	register
A	ⓝ 등산(登山)(하)	mountain climbing
B	ⓝ 등산로(登山路)[-노]	a path up a mountain
C	ⓝ 등장(登場)(하)	entry

C ⓥ	등장하다(登場-)	appear
C ⓝ	디스크(disk)	❶ disc ❷ disk
B ⓝ	디자이너(designer)	designer
B ⓝ	디자인(design)(하)	design
C ⓝ	따님	your (his) esteemed daughter
B ⓥ	따다	❶ pick ❷ cut out
A ⓐ	따뜻하다[-뜨타-]	(be) warm
B ⓥ	따라가다	follow
C ⓥ	따라다니다	follow about
C ⓓ	따라서	therefore
B ⓥ	따라오다	follow
B ⓓ	따로	separately
C ⓓ	따로따로	one by one
B ⓥ	따르다	pour
B ⓥ	따르다	❶ accompany ❷ chase after ❸ keep step with
C ⓐ	따스하다	(be) warm
B ⓓ	딱	accurately
C ⓓ	딱	❶ resolutely

		❷ entirely
		❸ perfectly
C	ⓐ 딱딱하다[-따카-]	❶ (be) hard
		❷ (be) stiff
B	ⓡ 딴	another
A	ⓝ 딸	daughter
A	ⓝ 딸기	strawberry
C	ⓝ 딸아이[따라-]	my daughter
B	ⓝ 땀	sweat
B	ⓝ 땅	earth
C	ⓝ 땅바닥[-빠-]	ground
C	ⓝ 땅속[-쏙]	underground
B	ⓝ 땅콩	peanut
A	ⓝ 때	❶ hour ❷ period
		❸ opportunity
C	ⓝ 때	dirt
B	ⓓ 때때로	sometimes
C	ⓓ 때로	sometimes
C	ⓥ 때리다	strike
A	ⓝ 때문	reason
B	ⓝ 땜	escape from bad

		luck
C	ⓥ 떠나가다	leave
A	ⓥ 떠나다	❶ leave
		❷ pass away
		❸ cut off
C	ⓥ 떠나오다	come back
B	ⓥ 떠들다	❶ be noisy
		❷ lift the corner of
C	ⓐ 떠들썩하다[-써카-]	❶ (be) noisy
		❷ (be) abroad <rumor>
B	ⓥ 떠오르다	❶ rise ❷ hit upon
B	ⓥ 떠올리다	recall
A	ⓝ 떡	rice cake
C	ⓝ 떡국[-꾹]	rice-cake soup
B	ⓝ 떡볶이[-뽀끼]	broiled dish of sliced rice cake, eggs, seasoning, etc.
B	ⓥ 떨다	tremble

B	v 떨리다	tremble
B	v 떨어뜨리다[떠러-]	❶ let fall
		❷ lower (head)
B	v 떨어지다[떠러-]	❶ drop
		❷ fail
		❸ go down (temperature)
C	n 떼	herd
B	v 떼다	❶ take off
		❷ keep apart
		❸ refuse
A	d 또	again
B	d 또는	or
B	d 또다시	once more
B	d 또한	❶ also ❷ and
A	a 똑같다[-깓따]	(be) just alike
B	d 똑같이[-까치]	equally
B	a 똑똑하다[-또카-]	❶ (be) clear
		❷ (be) smart
A	d 똑바로[-빠-]	❶ correctly
		❷ straight

B	ⓝ 뚜껑	lid
C	ⓥ 뚫다[뚤타]	❶ punch
		❷ penetrate
B	ⓐ 뚱뚱하다	(be) fat
C	ⓥ 뛰놀다	jump about
A	ⓥ 뛰다	(heart) beat
A	ⓥ 뛰다	run
C	ⓥ 뛰어가다	run
B	ⓥ 뛰어나가다	run forward
C	ⓐ 뛰어나다	(be) distinguished or eminent
C	ⓥ 뛰어나오다	bounce about
C	ⓥ 뛰어내리다	jump down
C	ⓥ 뛰어넘다[-따]	jump over
C	ⓥ 뛰어놀다	romp
B	ⓥ 뛰어다니다	run about
B	ⓥ 뛰어들다	jump into
B	ⓥ 뛰어오다	come running
C	ⓥ 뛰어오르다	❶ jump up
		❷ go up
A	ⓐ 뜨겁다[-따]	❶ (be) hot

		❷(be) burning
		❸(be) passionate
C	v 뜨다	go away
B	v 뜨다	❶open ❷emerse
B	v 뜨다	❶fly ❷rise
		❸float
C	v 뜯다[-따]	❶take away
		❷pick (seasoned vegetables)
C	n 뜰	yard
B	n 뜻[뜯]	❶will
		❷meaning
C	d 뜻대로[뜯때-]	in one's own way
C	n 뜻밖[뜯빡]	unexpectedness
C	d 뜻밖에[뜯빠께]	unexpectedly
C	v 뜻하다[뜨타-]	❶determine
		❷mean
C	v 띄다[띠-]	catch sight of
C	v 띄우다[띠-]	fly

ㄹ

A ⓝ 라디오(radio)	radio
A ⓝ 라면	instant noodle
C ⓝ 라운드(round)	round<boxing, golf>
C ⓝ 라이벌(rival)	❶ competitor ❷ rival
B ⓝ 라이터(lighter)	(cigarette) lighter
C ⓝ 라인(line)	line
C ⓝ 라켓(racket)[-켇]	racket (for tennis or badminton)
A ⓝ 러시아(Russia)	Russia
B ⓝ 런던(London)	London
B ⓝ 레몬(lemon)	lemon
B ⓝ 레스토랑(프restaurant)	restaurant
C ⓝ 레이저(laser)	laser
C ⓝ 레저(leisure)	❶ leisure ❷ entertainment
B ⓝ 렌즈(lens)	lens
C ⓝ 로봇(robot)[-볻]	robot

C ⓝ 로터리(rotary)	traffic circle
C ⓝ 리(里)	unit of distance (393m)
C ⓝ 리그(league)	athletic associations
B ⓝ 리듬(rhythm)	rhythm
C ⓝ 리터(liter)	liter

ㅁ

B	d 마구	① rashly ② carelessly
C	n 마누라	one's wife
B	n 마늘	garlic
C	n 마당	garden
C	n 마당	occasion
C	n 마디	① joint ② phrase
C	a 마땅하다	① (be) suitable ② ought to
C	n 마라톤(marathon)	marathon
C	n 마련	certainty
C	n 마련(하)	preparation
B	v 마련되다	be prepared
B	v 마련하다	prepare
B	n 마루	(wooden) floor
B	v 마르다	① dry ② become thin
A	n 마리	counting unit of animals

C	ⓝ 마무리(하)	finish
B	ⓝ 마사지(massage)(하)	massage
A	ⓥ 마시다	drink
C	ⓝ 마약(痲藥)	narcotic (ex. opium, heroin)
C	ⓝ 마요네즈(프mayonnaise)	mayonnaise
B	ⓝ 마을	village
A	ⓝ 마음	mind
C	ⓝ 마음가짐	resolution
C	ⓓ 마음껏[-껃]	to one's heart's content
B	ⓓ 마음대로	as one pleases
C	ⓥ 마음먹다[-따]	make up one's mind
B	ⓝ 마음속[-쏙]	one's mind
C	ⓝ 마음씨	temper
C	ⓝ 마이크(mike)	microphone
B	ⓓ 마주	face to face
C	ⓥ 마주치다	❶ crash with ❷ come across
B	ⓝ 마중(하)	reception

156

A	ⓝ 마지막	end
B	ⓝ 마찬가지	sameness
C	ⓝ 마찰(摩擦)(하)	rubbing
B	ⓓ 마치	as if
B	ⓥ 마치다	complete
B	ⓓ 마침	in the (very) nick of time
B	ⓓ 마침내	finally
C	ⓝ 마크(mark)	mark
A	ⓤ 마흔	forty
B	ⓓ 막	just now
B	ⓓ 막	random
C	ⓝ 막걸리[-껄-]	raw rice wine
B	ⓝ 막내[망-]	the youngest of the family
B	ⓥ 막다[-따]	❶ defend ❷ keep away
C	ⓓ 막상[-쌍]	ultimately
B	ⓥ 막히다[마키-]	❶ discontinue ❷ be blocked
C	ⓝ 만	time

C n	만	as many as
B r	만(滿)	enough
A r	만(萬)	ten thousand
A u	만(萬)	ten thousand
A v	만나다	❶ come across ❷ meet
B n	만남	meeting
B n	만두	dumpling
A v	만들다	❶ manufacture ❷ frame
B v	만들어지다[-드러-]	be made
C a	만만하다	❶ (be) easygoing ❷ (be) negligible
C n	만세(萬歲)	eternity
B n	만약(萬若)[마냑]	if
B n	만일(萬一)[마닐]	if
C n	만점(滿點)[-쩜]	full marks
C n	만족(滿足)(하)	satisfactory
C a	만족스럽다(滿足-)[-따]	(be) satisfactory
B v	만족하다(滿足-)[-조카-]	be satisfied with
B a	만족하다(滿足-)[-조카-]	(be) satisfied

B ⓥ 만지다	❶ touch ❷ handle
B ⓝ 만큼	❶ as…as
	❷ how much
C Ⓢ 만하다	❶ be enough to
	❷ be (well) worth doing
B ⓝ 만화(漫畵)	cartoon
C ⓝ 만화가(漫畵家)	cartoonist
A ⓐ 많다[만타]	(be) many
B ⓥ 많아지다[마나-]	get more quantity
A ⓓ 많이[마니]	much
B ⓝ 말	horse
B ⓝ 말(末)	end
A ⓝ 말(하)	talk
C ⓝ 말기(末期)	❶ last stage
	❷ old age
C ⓥ 말다	roll
A ⓥ 말다	cease
A Ⓢ 말다	❶ unnecessary
	❷ must not
C ⓥ 말리다	dehydrate

C	v 말리다	propitiate
A	n 말씀(하)	words
B	v 말씀드리다	honorific of tell (to eldership)
A	v 말씀하다	honorific of tell
C	d 말없이[마럽씨]	without a word
C	n 말투(-套)	❶way of speaking(tone) ❷accent
A	v 말하다	speak
A	a 맑다[막따]	❶(be) bright ❷(be) clear ❸(be) clean
C	n 맘	mind
C	d 맘대로	as one likes
A	n 맛[맏]	taste
C	v 맛보다[맏뽀-]	taste
A	a 맛없다[마덥따]	(be) tasteless
A	a 맛있다[마싣따]	(be) delicious
C	v 망설이다[-서리-]	hesitate
C	n 망원경(望遠鏡)	telescope

C	ⓥ 망치다	spoil
C	ⓥ 망하다(亡-)	❶perish ❷go bankrupt ❸be wretched
B	ⓥ 맞다[맏따]	correct
B	ⓥ 맞다[맏따]	be whipped
B	ⓥ 맞다[맏따]	welcome
B	ⓥ 맞서다[맏써-]	❶face each other ❷defy
B	ⓝ 맞은편(-便)[마즌-]	opposite side
C	ⓥ 맞이하다[마지-]	welcome
B	ⓥ 맞추다[맏-]	❶assemble ❷conform
B	ⓥ 맡기다[맏끼-]	entrust (a person) with
B	ⓥ 맡다[맏따]	take charge of
C	ⓥ 맡다[맏따]	smell
C	ⓝ 매	whip
C	ⓝ 매너(manner)	❶behavior ❷manners
B	ⓓ 매년(每年)	annually

B	ⓥ 매다	tie
C	ⓓ 매달(每-)	monthly
C	ⓥ 매달다	hang
C	ⓥ 매달리다	❶ be entangled
		❷ depend on
		❸ stick to
B	ⓝ 매력(魅力)	charm
C	ⓓ 매번(每番)	every time
C	ⓝ 매스컴	mass communication
A	ⓓ 매우	very
A	ⓝⓓ 매일(每日)	every day
C	ⓝ 매장(賣場)	counter<store>
C	ⓓ 매주(每週)	every week
C	ⓝ 매체(媒體)	media
A	ⓝ 맥주(麥酒)[-쭈]	beer
B	ⓡ 맨	the very
A	ⓐ 맵다[-따]	❶ (be) hot
		❷ (be) severe <weather>
C	ⓥ 맺다[맫따]	❶ contract

		② finish
A	n 머리	head
C	n 머리말	preface
B	n 머리카락	hair (of one's head)
C	n 머리칼	abbr. of hair
B	n 머릿속[-리쏙]	in one's head
B	v 머무르다	stay
C	v 머물다	abbr. of stay
C	v 먹고살다[-꼬-]	make one's livelihood
C	v 먹다[-따]	be deaf
A	s 먹다[-따]	completion (of act, state)
A	v 먹다[-따]	eat
C	n 먹이[머기]	prey
B	v 먹이다[머기-]	feed
B	v 먹히다[머키-]	be eaten
A	d 먼저	ahead
B	n 먼지	dust
A	a 멀다	(be) far
B	d 멀리	far away

B	v 멀어지다[머러-]	become more distant
B	v 멈추다	stop
B	n 멋[먿]	stylishness
B	a 멋있다[머싣따]	(be) handsome
C	a 멋지다[먿찌-]	(be) splendid
C	d 멍멍	bowwow
C	v 멎다[먿따]	stop
A	n 메뉴(menu)	menu
B	v 메다	carry on one's shoulder
B	n 메모(memo)(하)	memo
B	n 메시지(message)	message
C	v 메우다	let carry on one's shoulder
B	n 메일(mail)	e-mail
B	n 며느리	daughter-in-law
A	n 며칠	a few days
C	n 면(綿)	cotton
C	n 면(面)	side
C	n 면(面)	myeon <adminis-

		trative district>
C n	면담(面談)(하)	personal conversation
C n	면적(面積)	size (of a land)
C n	면접(面接)(하)	interview
C v	면하다(免-)	avoid
C n	멸치	anchovy
A n	명(名)	persons
C n	명단(名單)	list of names
B n	명령(命令)(하)[-녕]	command
C n	명령어(命令語)[-녕-]	command word
C n	명예(名譽)	honor
C n	명의(名義)[-이]	name
B n	명절(名節)	festival days
C n	명칭(名稱)	title
B n	명함(名銜)	name card
C a	명확하다(明確-)[-화카-]	(be) clear and accurate
A r	몇[면]	a few
B r	몇몇[면면]	several
B r	몇십[면씹]	several tens

C	ⓞ 모(某)	someone or something
C	ⓡ 모(某)	Mr. so and so
C	ⓝ 모금	sip
B	ⓝ 모기	mosquito
B	ⓝ 모니터(monitor)	monitor <computer>
B	ⓝ 모델(model)	(fashion) model
A	ⓓ 모두	❶ total ❷ everybody
A	ⓝ 모두	all
A	ⓡ 모든	all
B	ⓝ 모래	sand
B	ⓝ 모레	the day after tomorrow
A	ⓥ 모르다	fail to notice
C	ⓝ 모범(模範)	example
C	ⓥ 모색하다(摸索-)[-새카-]	grope
B	ⓝ 모습	appearance
B	ⓥ 모시다	❶ serve ❷ accompany

B	n 모양(模樣)	shape
B	n 모양(模樣)	signs, indication
C	v 모여들다	gather
B	v 모으다	❶collect ❷gather (people)
B	v 모이다	gather
B	n 모임	gathering
A	n 모자(帽子)	cap
B	v 모자라다	lack
C	d 모조리	wholly
C	n 모집(募集)(하)	recruitment
C	v 모집하다(募集-)[-지파-]	recruit
C	d 모처럼	after a long time
C	n 모퉁이	corner
A	n 목	neck
B	n 목걸이[-꺼리]	necklace
C	n 목록(目錄)[몽녹]	list
B	n 목사(牧師)[-싸]	pastor
B	n 목소리[-쏘-]	❶voice ❷shout
C	n 목숨[-쑴]	life
A	n 목요일(木曜日)[모교-]	Thursday

A	n 목욕(沐浴)(하)[모곡]	bathing
B	n 목욕탕(沐浴湯)[모곡-]	bathhouse
B	n 목적(目的)[-쩍]	aim
B	n 목표(目標)	target
B	v 몰다	❶ chase (animal) ❷ drive (a car)
B	d 몰래	secretly
C	v 몰려들다	come in crowds
C	v 몰려오다	come in crowds
A	n 몸	body
C	n 몸매	one's shape or figure
B	n 몸무게	(body) weight
B	n 몸살	illness from fatigue
C	n 몸속[-쏙]	interior of the body
C	n 몸짓(하)[-찓]	gesture
C	n 몸통	bulk of one's body
B	d 몹시[-씨]	severely
A	d 못[몯]	not
C	n 못[몯]	nail
C	a 못되다[몯뙤-]	(be) evil

C ⓐ 못생기다[몯쌩-]	(be) ugly
C ⓐ 못지않다[몯찌안타]	(be) no less than
A Ⓥ 못하다[모타-]	cannot
A ⓐ 못하다[모타-]	(be) inferior
A Ⓢ 못하다[모타-]	be impossible
C ⓝ 묘사(描寫)(하)	description
C Ⓥ 묘사하다(描寫-)	describe
B ⓝ 무	radish
C ⓝ 무(無)	nonexistence
A ⓐ 무겁다[-따]	❶(be) heavy
	❷(be) serious <punishment>
B ⓝ 무게	❶weight
	❷dignity
C ⓝ 무관심(無關心)(하)	indifference
C ⓐ 무관심하다(無關心-)	(be) indifferent
C ⓝ 무궁화(無窮花)	rose of Sharon (national flower of Korea)
C ⓝ 무기(武器)	weapon
C Ⓥ 무너지다	collapse

B	ⓝ무늬[-니]	pattern
C	ⓝ무대(舞臺)	stage
B	ⓝ무더위	sweltering weather
C	ⓝ무덤	tomb
C	ⓐ무덥다[-따]	(be) sultry
C	ⓓ무려(無慮)	as many as
B	ⓝ무렵	about the time
C	ⓝ무료(無料)	no charge
B	ⓝ무릎[-릅]	knee
C	ⓝ무리	throng
C	ⓝ무리(無理)(하)	unreasonableness
C	ⓐ무리하다(無理-)	❶(be) unreasonable ❷(be) excessive
C	ⓐ무사하다(無事-)	(be) safe
B	ⓐ무섭다[-따]	❶(be) fearful ❷(be) scared ❸(be) awful
A	ⓡ무슨	what
B	ⓥ무시하다(無視-)	neglect
B	ⓞ무어	what

A	ⓞ 무엇[-얻]	what
B	ⓝ 무역(貿易)(하)	(foreign) trade
B	ⓝ 무용(舞踊)(하)	dancing
C	ⓝ 무용가(舞踊家)	dancer
C	ⓐ 무의미하다(無意味-)	(be) meaningless
B	ⓓ 무조건(無條件)[-껀]	unconditional
C	ⓝ 무지개	rainbow
C	ⓐ 무책임하다(無責任-)[-채김-]	(be) irresponsible
B	ⓓ 무척	extremely
C	ⓥ 묵다[-따]	stay at (a hotel)
C	ⓥ 묵다[-따]	get out-of-date
B	ⓥ 묶다[묵따]	❶ fasten ❷ join together
C	ⓥ 묶이다[무끼-]	be fastened
A	ⓝ 문(門)	door
C	ⓝ 문구(文句)[-꾸]	words
C	ⓓ 문득[-뜩]	suddenly
C	ⓝ 문밖(門-)[-박]	outside of a house
C	ⓝ 문법(文法)[-뻡]	grammar
C	ⓝ 문서(文書)	document

C	n 문자(文字)[-짜]	letters
B	n 문장(文章)	❶ sentence
		❷ writing
A	n 문제(問題)	❶ question
		❷ trouble
C	v 문제되다(問題-)	come into question
B	n 문제점(問題點)[-쩜]	point at issue
B	n 문학(文學)	literature
C	n 문학적(文學的))[-쩍]	literary
B	n 문화(文化)	culture
C	n 문화재(文化財)	cultural assets
C	n 문화적(文化的)	cultural
C	v 묻다[-따]	bury
A	v 묻다[-따]	ask
B	v 묻다[-따]	be stained
C	v 묻히다[무치-]	get buried
C	v 묻히다[무치-]	smear
A	n 물	water
C	n 물가(物價)[-까]	prices
A	n 물건(物件)	goods
C	n 물결[-껼]	wave

B	ⓝ 물고기[-꼬-]	fish
C	ⓝ 물기[-끼]	moisture
B	ⓥ 물다	bite
C	ⓥ 물러나다	❶ withdraw
		❷ get out of place
A	ⓝⓓ 물론(勿論)	needless to say
C	ⓝ 물리학(物理學)	physics
B	ⓝ 물속[-쏙]	underwater
A	ⓥ 물어보다[무러-]	ask (questions)
B	ⓝ 물음[무름]	question
C	ⓝ 물질(物質)[-찔]	substance or material
C	ⓝ 물질적(物質的)[-찔-]	physical
C	ⓝ 물체(物體)	object
A	ⓔ 뭐	what
A	ⓞ 뭐	what
C	ⓔ 뭘	what
C	ⓞ 뭣[뭘]	what
C	ⓝ 미(美)	beauty
A	ⓝ 미국(美國)	U.S.A.
C	ⓥ 미끄러지다	❶ slide

Korean Essential Vocabulary 6000

		❷ fail (in an exam)
C	ⓐ 미끄럽다[-따]	(be) slippery
C	ⓝ 미니(mini)	mini
B	ⓝ 미디어(media)	media
B	ⓝ 미래(未來)	future
C	ⓥ 미루다	❶ put off
		❷ shift (the blame on a person)
B	ⓓ 미리	advance
C	ⓝ 미만(未滿)	less than
C	ⓝ 미사일(missile)	missile
B	ⓝ 미소(微笑)(하)	smile
B	ⓝ 미술(美術)	art
B	ⓝ 미술관(美術館)	art gallery
C	ⓝ 미스(Miss)	Miss
A	ⓐ 미안하다(未安-)	(be) sorry
C	ⓝ 미역	brown seaweed
C	ⓝ 미용실(美容室)	beauty salon
C	ⓝ 미움	hatred
B	ⓥ 미워하다	hate
B	ⓝ 미인(美人)	beautiful woman

C	d 미처	(not) up to that
B	v 미치다	reach
B	v 미치다	❶ go mad
		❷ come up to (the standard)
A	n 미터(meter)	meter
B	n 미팅(meeting)(하)	❶ date with other sex
		❷ meeting
C	n 미혼(未婚)	unmarried
C	n 민간(民間)	nongovernmental
C	n 민속(民俗)	ethnic customs
B	n 민족(民族)	peoples
C	n 민주(民主)	popular rule
C	n 민주주의(民主主義)	democracy
C	n 민주화(民主化)	democratization
B	v 믿다[-따]	❶ trust
		❷ believe in
C	v 믿어지다[미더-]	believe
B	n 믿음[미듬]	❶ trust ❷ faith
B	n 밀가루[-까-]	flour

B	ⓥ밀다	push
C	ⓥ밀리다	❶be left undone ❷be pushed (in competition)
B	ⓝ밀리미터(millimeter)	millimeter
C	ⓐ밀접하다(密接-)[-쩌파-]	(be) close
B	ⓐ밉다[-따]	❶(be) hateful ❷(be) ugly
B	ⓓ및[믿]	and (also)
A	ⓝ밑[믿]	lower part
C	ⓝ밑바닥[믿빠-]	bottom

ㅂ

C	ⓝ 바	unit of pressure
C	ⓝ 바(bar)	bar
C	ⓝ 바가지	gourd
C	ⓝ 바구니	basket
B	ⓝ 바깥[- 깥]	outside
C	ⓝ 바깥쪽[- 깥-]	outside
A	ⓥ 바꾸다	change
B	ⓥ 바뀌다	get changed
A	ⓝ 바나나(banana)	banana
B	ⓝ 바늘	needle
A	ⓝ 바다	sea
B	ⓝ 바닥	❶ bottom ❷ foundation
B	ⓝ 바닷가[-다까]	beach
B	ⓝ 바닷물[-단-]	sea water
B	ⓥ 바라다	wish
B	ⓥ 바라보다	❶ look ❷ expect ❸ be getting on for
C	ⓝ 바람	desire

A	n 바람	wind
A	n 바람	cause
C	a 바람직하다[-지카-]	(be) desirable
A	d 바로	❶ right away
		❷ correctly
		❸ just like
C	v 바로잡다[-따]	❶ straighten
		❷ correct
B	v 바르다	paste
B	a 바르다	❶ (be) straight
		❷ (be) honest
B	n 바보	idiot
A	a 바쁘다	❶ (be) busy
		❷ (be) urgent
C	d 바싹	❶ parched
		❷ tightly
		❸ closely
B	n 바위	rock
C	n 바이러스(virus)	virus
B	n 바이올린(violin)	violin
A	n 바지	trousers

C	v 바치다	❶ pay ❷ devote
C	n 바퀴	turn of the wheel
C	n 바퀴	wheel
C	n 바탕	❶ basis ❷ quality
C	n 박(泊)	staying the night
C	v 박다[-따]	❶ hammer ❷ take (root)
A	n 박물관(博物館)[방-]	museum
B	n 박사(博士)[-싸]	Dr.
B	n 박수(拍手)(하)[-쑤]	handclap
B	n 박스(box)	box
C	v 박히다[바키-]	be nailed
A	n 밖[박]	outside
A	n 반(半)	half
A	n 반(班)	a group (company, class, party)
A	a 반갑다[-따]	(be) glad
C	v 반기다	rejoice
B	n 반대(反對)(하)	objection
C	n 반대편(反對便)	opposite side

B	v	반대하다(反對-)	object to
B	d	반드시	(most) certainly
C	n	반말(半-)	crude language
C	n	반면(反面)	other side
C	n	반발(反撥)(하)	❶ repulsion
			❷ resistance
C	v	반복되다(反復-)	repeat
B	v	반복하다(反復-)[-보카-]	switch again and again
C	n	반성(反省)(하)	reflection
C	v	반성하다(反省-)	introspect
C	v	반영하다(反映-)[바녕-]	reflect
C	n	반응(反應)(하)[바능]	reaction
B	n	반장	section leader
C	n	반죽(하)	❶ kneading
			❷ dough
B	n	반지(斑指)	ring
C	v	반짝거리다	glitter
C	v	반짝이다[-짜기-]	❶ twinkle
			❷ shine
B	n	반찬(飯饌)	(side) dish

B	Ⓥ 반하다(反-)	be against
A	Ⓥ 받다[-따]	❶ receive
		❷ take (an order)
		❸ accept ❹ suffer
		❺ support
B	Ⓥ 받아들이다[바다드리-]	❶ absorb
		❷ permit
B	Ⓝ 받침	❶ prop
		❷ final consonant
A	Ⓝ 발	foot
B	Ⓝ 발가락[-까-]	toe
C	Ⓝ 발걸음[-꺼름]	pace
B	Ⓝ 발견(發見)(하)	discovery
B	Ⓥ 발견되다(發見-)	be discovered
B	Ⓥ 발견하다(發見-)	discover
C	Ⓝ 발길[-낄]	kick
C	Ⓝ 발끝[-끋]	tiptoe
B	Ⓝ 발달(發達)(하)[-딸]	development
C	Ⓥ 발달되다(發達-)[-딸-]	grow
B	Ⓥ 발달하다(發達-)[-딸-]	grow
B	Ⓝ 발등[-뜽]	top of the foot

C	n 발레(ballet)	ballet
B	n 발목	ankle
C	n 발바닥[-빠-]	sole of the foot
B	n 발생(發生)(하)[-쌩]	happening
B	v 발생하다(發生-)[-쌩-]	be generated
A	n 발음(發音)(하)[바름]	pronunciation
B	v 발음하다(發音-)[바름-]	pronounce
C	n 발자국[-짜-]	footprint
B	n 발전(發展)(하)[-쩐]	development
C	n 발전(發電)(하)[-쩐]	generation of electric power
C	v 발전되다(發展-)[-쩐-]	be developed
B	v 발전하다(發展-)[-쩐-]	develop
C	n 발톱	toenail
B	n 발표(發表)(하)	presentation
C	v 발표되다(發表-)	be announced
B	v 발표하다(發表-)	announce
C	v 발휘하다(發揮-)	display
B	v 밝다[박따]	dawn
A	a 밝다[박따]	(be) bright
C	v 밝아지다[발가-]	brighten

C	ⓥ 밝혀내다 [발켜-]	trace
C	ⓥ 밝혀지다 [발켜-]	be traced
B	ⓥ 밝히다 [발키-]	❶ stay up (all night) ❷ light (up) ❸ clarify ❹ be crazed about (a person)
B	ⓥ 밟다 [밥따]	❶ step ❷ trail ❸ go through (a course)
B	ⓝ 밤	chestnut
A	ⓝ 밤(夜)	night
B	ⓝ 밤낮 [-낟]	❶ night and day ❷ always
B	ⓐ 밤늦다 [-늗따]	(be) late at night
C	ⓝ 밤새 [-쌔]	night time
B	ⓥ 밤새다	sit up all night
C	ⓥ 밤새우다	sit up all night
C	ⓝ 밤색(-色)	chestnut color
B	ⓝ 밤중(-中) [-쭝]	midnight

C	n 밤하늘	night sky
A	n 밥(飯)	boiled rice
B	n 밥그릇[-끄륻]	rice bowl
B	n 밥맛[밤맏]	❶flavor of rice ❷appetite
C	n 밥상(-床)[-쌍]	eating table
B	n 밥솥[-쏟]	rice-cooker
A	n 방(房)	room
B	d 방금(方今)	just now
C	n 방면(方面)	direction
B	n 방문(房門)	door of a room
B	n 방문(訪問)(하)	visit
B	v 방문하다(訪問-)	visit
C	n 방바닥(房-)[-빠-]	floor of a room
B	n 방법(方法)	method
B	n 방송(放送)(하)	broadcasting
B	n 방송국(放送局)	broadcasting station
C	n 방송사(放送社)	broadcasting station
C	v 방송하다(放送-)	broadcast

C	n 방식(方式)	method
C	n 방안(方案)	plan
C	n 방울	drop
C	n 방울	bell
C	n 방지(防止)(하)	prevention
C	v 방지하다(防止-)	block
A	n 방학(放學)(하)	vacation
C	n 방해(妨害)(하)	disturbance
C	v 방해하다(妨害-)	disturb
B	n 방향(方向)	direction
B	n 밭[받]	farm
A	n 배	abdoment
A	n 배	pear
A	n 배	ship
C	n 배(倍)	times
B	n 배경(背景)	❶ background
		❷ support
		❸ setting
A	a 배고프다	(be) hungry
B	n 배구(排球)	volleyball
B	n 배꼽	❶ navel

		❷ calyx of a fruit
C	ⓥ 배다	soak into
B	ⓝ 배달(配達)(하)	delivery
B	ⓝ 배드민턴(badminton)	badminton
A	ⓐ 배부르다	(be) full
B	ⓝ 배우(俳優)	actor or actress
A	ⓥ 배우다	learn
C	ⓝ 배우자(配偶者)	spouse
B	ⓝ 배추	Chinese cabbage
C	ⓝ 배추김치	pickled cabbage
C	ⓝ 배치(配置)(하)	❶ arrangement
		❷ distribution
A	ⓝ 백(百)	hundred
A	ⓤ 백(百)	hundred
C	ⓝ 백두산(白頭山)[-뚜-]	Mt.Baekdu
C	ⓝ 백색(白色)[-쌕]	white color
C	ⓝ 백성(百姓)[-썽]	people
C	ⓝ 백인(白人)[배긴]	Caucasian
C	ⓝ 백제(百濟)[-쩨]	Baekje \<one of ancient nations\>
A	ⓝ 백화점(百貨店)[배콰-]	department store

B	n 뱀	snake
C	n 뱃사람[배싸-]	sailor
C	v 뱉다[밷따]	spit out
C	v 버려지다	be discarded
B	n 버릇[-른]	habit
A	s 버리다	completion
B	v 버리다	❶ throw
		❷ destroy
		❸ (people) in ruins
B	n 버섯[-섣]	mushroom
A	n 버스(bus)	bus
B	n 버터(butter)	butter
B	n 버튼(button)	push button
C	v 버티다	❶ withstand
		❷ endure
A	n 번(番)	time
C	n 번개	lightning
C	a 번거롭다[-따]	(be) complicated
B	n 번역(飜譯)(하)[버녁]	translation
C	v 번역하다(飜譯-)[버녀카-]	translate
C	n 번지(番地)	house number

B	ⓝ 번째(番-)	~th, rd, st
A	ⓝ 번호(番號)	number
C	ⓝ 벌	bee
C	ⓝ 벌	suit (of clothes)
C	ⓝ 벌(罰)	punishment
C	ⓝ 벌금(罰金)	penalty
B	ⓥ 벌다	earn
C	ⓓ 벌떡	suddenly
B	ⓝ 벌레	insect
B	ⓥ 벌리다	outstretch
A	ⓓ 벌써	already
C	ⓥ 벌어지다[버러-]	enlarge
B	ⓥ 벌어지다[버러-]	crack apart
B	ⓥ 벌이다[버리-]	❶ spread ❷ set up ❸ start ❹ exhibit
C	ⓝ 범위(範圍)[버뷔]	range
C	ⓝ 범인(犯人)[버민]	criminal
C	ⓝ 범죄(犯罪)	crime
B	ⓝ 법(法)	law
C	ⓝ 법률(法律)[범뉼]	the law

C	n 법원(法院)[버붠]	courtroom
C	n 법적(法的)[-쩍]	legal
C	n 법칙(法則)	rule
B	v 벗기다[벋끼-]	❶ strip
		❷ uncover
		❸ take off
		❹ peel
A	v 벗다[벋따]	take off (clothes)
B	n 베개	pillow
C	v 베다	cut
B	n 베이징(北京)	Beijing
C	n 벤치(bench)	bench
B	n 벨트(belt)	❶ belt
		❷ (belt) conveyer
		❸ zone
C	n 벼	rice plant
B	n 벽(壁)	wall
C	n 변경(變更)(하)	modification
C	n 변동(變動)(하)	fluctuation
C	n 변명(辨明)(하)	excuse
C	n 변신(變身)(하)	disguise

B	ⓥ 변하다(變-)	become different
B	ⓝ 변호사(辯護士)	lawyer
B	ⓝ 변화(變化)(하)	change
C	ⓥ 변화되다(變化-)	change
B	ⓥ 변화하다(變化-)	change
A	ⓝ 별	star
B	ⓕ 별(別)	oddity
C	ⓐ 별다르다(別-)	(be) particular
C	ⓝ 별도(別途)[-또]	separate use
B	ⓓ 별로(別-)	especially
C	ⓝ 별명(別名)	nickname
C	ⓝ 별일(別-)[-릴]	❶ odd thing ❷ particular thing
A	ⓝ 병(瓶)	bottle
A	ⓝ 병(病)	disease
B	ⓥ 병들다(病-)	get sick
C	ⓝ 병실(病室)	sick room
C	ⓝ 병아리	chick
A	ⓝ 병원(病院)	hospital
B	ⓝ 보고(報告)(하)	briefing
B	ⓝ 보고서(報告書)	(written) report

C	ⓥ 보고하다(報告-)	report
C	ⓝ 보관(保管)(하)	safekeeping
B	ⓥ 보관하다(保管-)	keep
A	ⓥ 보내다	❶ dispatch (people) ❷ post (letter)
C	ⓥ 보내오다	deliver
C	ⓝ 보너스	bonus
A	ⓥ 보다	see
A	ⓢ 보다	try
A	ⓓ 보다	rather than
C	ⓝ 보도(報道)(하)	report
C	ⓥ 보도되다(報道-)	be reported
C	ⓥ 보도하다(報道-)	report
C	ⓝ 보라색(-色)	violet
B	ⓝ 보람	❶ sign ❷ symbol ❸ worth
C	ⓝ 보름	fifteenth day of a lunar month
C	ⓝ 보리	barley
C	ⓥ 보살피다	take care of

C	n	보상(補償)(하)	compensation
C	n	보수(保守)(하)	conservation
C	n	보수(補修)(하)	repair
C	n	보수적(保守的)	conservative
C	n	보안(保安)(하)	preservation of public peace
C	v	보완하다(補完-)	complement
B	v	보이다	show
B	v	보이다	be seen
C	n	보자기(褓-)	wrapping cloth
C	n	보장(保障)(하)	guarantee
C	v	보장되다(保障-)	be guaranteed
C	v	보장하다(保障-)	guarantee
C	n	보전(保全)(하)	preservation <evidence, land>
C	n	보조(補助)(하)	assistance
C	n	보존(保存)(하)	maintenance <mass, energy>
C	v	보존하다(保存-)	preserve
C	v	보충하다(補充-)	supplement
A	n	보통(普通)	normality

B	d 보통(普通)	normal
C	n 보편적	universal
B	n 보험(保險)	insurance
B	n 보호(保護)(하)	protection
C	v 보호되다(保護-)	protect
C	v 보호하다(保護-)	protect
C	n 복(福)	(good) fortune
B	n 복도(複道)[-또]	corridor
B	n 복사(複寫)(하)[-싸]	copy
C	n 복사기(複寫機)[-싸-]	copy machine
B	v 복사하다(複寫-)[-싸-]	copy
C	n 복숭아[-쑹-]	peach
B	n 복습(復習)(하)[-씁]	review (lessons)
B	v 복습하다(復習-)[-쓰파-]	review (lessons)
A	a 복잡하다(複雜-)[-짜파-]	(be) complex
B	v 볶다[복따]	❶ parch ❷ torment
C	n 볶음[보끔]	roast
B	n 볶음밥[보끔-]	stir-fried rice
C	r 본(本)	current
C	n 본격적(本格的)[-껵쩍]	regular

B	n 본래(本來)[볼-]	originally
C	n 본부(本部)	headquarters
C	n 본사(本社)	❶ our company ❷ head office
C	n 본성(本性)	original nature
C	n 본인(本人)[보닌]	person himself
C	n 본질(本質)	essence
C	n 볼	cheek
C	n 볼링(bowling)	bowling
B	n 볼일[-릴]	job which must be done
A	n 볼펜(ball pen)	ball(-point) pen
A	n 봄	springtime
C	n 봉사(奉仕)(하)	service
C	v 봉사하다(奉仕-)	serve
B	n 봉지(封紙)	paper bag
B	n 봉투(封套)	envelope
B	v 뵈다	see humbly
B	v 뵈다	shorten word of be seen
B	v 뵙다[-따]	pay a formal visit

C	n 부(富)	wealth
C	n 부(父)	father
B	n 부(部)	copy (of a book)
B	n 부근(附近)	vicinity
B	n 부끄러움	❶ shyness
		❷ shame
B	a 부끄럽다[-따]	❶ (be) shy
		❷ (be) disgraceful
C	n 부담(負擔)(하)	charge
C	v 부담하다(負擔-)	pay
C	n 부대(部隊)	(military) unit
B	n 부동산(不動産)	real estate
B	a 부드럽다[-따]	❶ (be) soft
		❷ (be) gentle <temper, attitude>
B	v 부딪치다[-딛-]	collide with
C	v 부딪히다[-디치-]	be bumped into
B	v 부러워하다	envy
C	v 부러지다	break
B	a 부럽다[-따]	(be) enviable
A	v 부르다	call

B	ⓐ 부르다	(be) full
A	ⓝ 부모(父母)	parents
A	ⓝ 부모님(父母-)	honorific expression of parents
C	ⓝ 부문(部門)	section
A	ⓝ 부부(夫婦)	husband and wife
B	ⓝ 부분(部分)	part
C	ⓝ 부분적(部分的)	partial
A	ⓝ 부산(釜山)	Busan
C	ⓝ 부상(負傷)(하)	wound
C	ⓝ 부서(部署)	department <company>
C	ⓥ 부서지다	❶ break ❷ destroy ❸ ruin
A	ⓝ 부엌[-억]	kitchen
C	ⓝ 부위(部位)	part
A	ⓝ 부인(夫人)	wife
C	ⓝ 부인(婦人)	(married) woman
B	ⓝ 부자(富者)	rich person
B	ⓝ 부작용(副作用)[-자굥]	side effect
B	ⓝ 부잣집(富者-)[-자찝]	rich family

B	ⓝ 부장(部長)	department manager
C	ⓝ 부재(不在)(하)	absence
C	ⓝ 부정(不正)(하)	injustice
C	ⓝ 부정적	uncertain
C	ⓥ 부정하다(否定-)	deny
B	ⓝ 부족(部族)	tribe
B	ⓝ 부족(不正)(하)	shortage
B	ⓐ 부족하다(不足-)[-조카-]	(be) insufficient
B	ⓐ 부지런하다	(be) diligent
C	ⓓ 부지런히	diligently
C	ⓝ 부채	folding fan
B	ⓝ 부처	Buddha
B	ⓥ 부치다	mail
C	ⓝ 부친(父親)	father
B	ⓝ 부탁(付託)(하)	favor
B	ⓥ 부탁하다(付託-)[-타카-]	ask a favor
C	ⓝ 부품(部品)	parts
C	ⓝ 부피	bulk
C	ⓝ 부회장(副會長)	vice-chairman
B	ⓝ 북(北)	north

C	ⓝ 북부(北部)[-뿌]	northern part
A	ⓝ 북쪽(北-)	north
B	ⓝ 북한(北韓)[부칸]	North Korea
A	ⓝ 분	one-tenth
A	ⓝ 분(分)	minute
C	ⓝ 분노(憤怒)(하)	anger
C	ⓝ 분량(分量)[불-]	quantity
C	ⓝ 분리(分離)(하)[불-]	separation
C	ⓥ 분리되다(分離-)[불-]	be divided
C	ⓥ 분리하다(分離-)[불-]	divide
B	ⓓ 분명(分明)(하)	clearly
C	ⓐ 분명하다(分明-)	(be) clear
C	ⓥ 분명해지다(分明-)	get clear
B	ⓓ 분명히(分明-)	plainly
C	ⓝ 분석(分析)(하)	analysis
B	ⓥ 분석하다(分析-)[-서카-]	analyze
C	ⓝ 분야(分野)[부냐]	field
B	ⓝ 분위기(雰圍氣)[부뉘-]	atmosphere
C	ⓐ 분주하다(奔走-)	(be) busy
C	ⓥ 분포하다(分布-)	be distributed
C	ⓝ 분필(粉筆)	chalk

C	ⓝ 분홍색(粉紅色)	pink
A	ⓝ 불(火)	fire
B	ⓐ 불가능하다(不可能-)(하)	(be) impossible
C	ⓐ 불가피하다(不可避-)(하)	(be) inevitable
A	ⓝ 불고기	bulgogi, roast meat (sliced and seasoned)
C	ⓓ 불과(不過)(하)	merely
C	ⓐ 불과하다(不過-)	(be) nothing but
B	ⓝ 불교(佛敎)	Buddhism
C	ⓥ 불구하다(不拘-)	disregard
B	ⓝ 불꽃[-꼳]	spark
A	ⓥ 불다	blow
C	ⓥ 불러일으키다[-이르-]	❶ rouse up ❷ arouse
C	ⓥ 불리다	soak (in the water)
B	ⓥ 불리다	be called
C	ⓐ 불리하다(不利-)	(be) disadvantageous
B	ⓝ 불만(不滿)(하)	dissatisfaction
C	ⓝ 불법(不法)(하)[-뻡]	unlawfulness

C	n 불법(佛法)[-뻡]	teaching of Buddha
B	n 불빛[-삗]	flame color
B	a 불쌍하다	(be) pitiable
B	n 불안(不安)(하)[부란]	uneasiness
B	a 불안하다(不安-)[부란-]	(be) nervous
C	v 불어오다[부러-]	blow in
C	a 불완전하다(不完全-)	(be) imperfect
C	n 불이익(不利益)[-리-]	drawback
C	n 불편(不便)(하)	❶ inconvenience ❷ discomfort
B	a 불편하다(不便)	❶ (be) inconvenient ❷ (be) uncomfortable
C	n 불평(不平)(하)	complaint
C	a 불평등하다(不平等-)	(be) unequal
C	a 불필요하다(不必要)[-피료-]	(be) unnecessary
C	n 불행(不幸)(하)	unhappiness
B	a 불행하다(不幸)	(be) unhappy

C	ⓐ 불확실하다(不確實-)[-씰-]	(be) uncertain
B	ⓐ 붉다[북따]	(be) red
C	ⓐ 붐비다	❶ (be) jammed
		❷ (be) crowded
B	ⓥ 붓다[붇따]	swell
C	ⓥ 붓다[붇따]	pour
B	ⓥ 붙다[붇따]	❶ stick to
		❷ be close
		❸ fight
		❹ depend on
		❺ pass the exam
		❻ start
		❼ be parasitic
		❽ attach
		❾ form ❿ have
		⓫ acquire
		⓬ nursing
		⓭ catch (fire)
C	ⓥ 붙들다[붇뜰-]	❶ catch ❷ start
		❸ capture ❹ help
B	ⓥ 붙이다[부치-]	❶ attach ❷ light

		❸ give a name
		❹ bet
		❺ place close to
C	ⓥ 붙잡다[붇짭따]	❶ seize ❷ get
		❸ catch
C	ⓥ 붙잡히다[붇짜피-]	be caught
C	ⓝ 브랜드(brand)	brand
B	ⓝ 블라우스(blouse)	blouse
A	ⓝ 비	rain
C	ⓝ 비(碑)	tombstone
B	ⓝ 비교(比較)(하)	comparison
B	ⓓ 비교적(比較的)	relatively
B	ⓥ 비교하다(比較-)	compare
C	ⓝ 비극(悲劇)	tragedy
C	ⓥ 비기다	compare to
C	ⓝ 비난(非難)(하)	criticism
A	ⓝ 비누	soap
B	ⓝ 비닐(vinyl)	vinyl
B	ⓝ 비닐봉지(vinyl封紙)	vinyl paper bag
C	ⓥ 비다	empty
C	ⓝ 비둘기	dove

A	ⓝ 비디오(video)	video
C	ⓓ 비로소	not…until
C	ⓥ 비롯되다[-롣뙤-]	originate
C	ⓥ 비롯하다[-로타-]	headed by
C	ⓝ 비만(肥滿)	fatness
C	ⓝ 비명(悲鳴)	scream
B	ⓝ 비밀(秘密)	secret
C	ⓝ 비바람	rainstorm
C	ⓥ 비비다	❶ rub ❷ mix
A	ⓝ 비빔밥[-빱]	boiled rice with assorted mixtures
C	ⓝ 비상(非常)	❶ emergency ❷ extraordinarness
B	ⓝ 비서(秘書)	secretary
A	ⓐ 비슷하다[-스타-]	(be) similar
A	ⓐ 비싸다	(be) expensive
B	ⓝ 비용(費用)	cost
C	ⓥ 비우다	make empty
C	ⓥ 비웃다[-욷따]	laugh
C	ⓝ 비율(比率)	rate
C	ⓝ 비중(比重)	relative impor-

		tance
C	v 비추다	❶ shine ❷ flash ❸ reflect ❹ compare (with)
C	v 비치다	❶ shine ❷ be reflected ❸ show
B	v 비키다	❶ make room for·· ❷ move ❸ avoid
B	n 비타민(vitamin)	vitamin
C	n 비판(批判)(하)	❶ comment ❷ criticism
C	n 비판적(批判的)	critical
B	v 비판하다(批判-)	criticize
C	v 비하다(比-)	compare
C	n 비행(非行)	misconduct
C	n 비행(飛行)(하)	flying
A	n 비행기(飛行機)	airplane
C	n 비행장(飛行場)	airfield
B	v 빌다	❶ beg ❷ pray, wish

B	n 빌딩(building)	building
B	v 빌리다	❶ lend
		❷ adopt (format)
B	n 빗[빋]	comb
B	n 빗물[빈-]	rainwater
C	n 빗방울[비빵-]	raindrops
C	n 빗줄기[비쭐-]	great streaks of rain
C	n 빚[빋]	debt
B	n 빛[빋]	❶ light
		❷ color
C	n 빛깔[빋-]	color
C	v 빛나다[빈-]	❶ shine
		❷ luster
		❸ shine briliantly
C	v 빠뜨리다	❶ omit ❷ tempt
A	a 빠르다	(be) fast
C	v 빠져나가다	sneak away (from)
C	v 빠져나오다	come out (of a room)
B	v 빠지다	fall out <tooth, fur>

B	ⓥ 빠지다	fall
A	ⓝ 빨간색(-色)	red
B	ⓐ 빨갛다[-가타]	(be) red
C	ⓥ 빨다	sip
B	ⓥ 빨다	wash
B	ⓝ 빨래(하)	❶ laundry ❷ washing
A	ⓓ 빨리	quickly
A	ⓝ 빵	bread
C	ⓥ 빼놓다[-노타]	❶ leave (a person) ❷ draw out
B	ⓥ 빼다	pull out
C	ⓥ 빼앗기다[-앗끼-]	be taken away
C	ⓥ 빼앗다[-앋따]	take away
C	ⓥ 뺏다[뺃따]	abbr. of take away
B	ⓝ 뺨	❶ cheeks ❷ edge
C	ⓢ 뻔하다	(be) unquestionable
C	ⓐ 뻔하다	emphatic variant of be clear

B	v	뻗다[-따]	① emphatic variant of spread
			② slang of die
B	n	뼈	① bone
			② main points
B	v	뽑다[-따]	① pull out
			② extend
			③ draw out
			④ eradicate
			⑤ select
C	v	뽑히다[뽀피-]	be pulled out
B	n	뿌리	① root
			② origin
B	v	뿌리다	① sprinkle(snow)
			② sprinkle
			③ spend money freely
C	v	뿌리치다	① shake off (a person's grasp)
			② refuse
B	n	뿐	only

ㅅ

A	ⓤ 사(四)	four
C	ⓝ 사건(事件)[-껀]	case
B	ⓝ 사계절(四季節)	four seasons
B	ⓝ 사고(事故)	accident
C	ⓝ 사고(思考)(하)	thinking
A	ⓝ 사과(沙果)	apple
C	ⓝ 사과(謝過)(하)	apology
B	ⓥ 사과하다(謝過-)	apologize
C	ⓥ 사귀다	make friends with
C	ⓝ 사기(士氣)	fighting spirit
C	ⓝ 사나이	man
C	ⓝ 사냥(하)	hunting
A	ⓥ 사다	❶ buy
		❷ sell for(money)
		❸ incur
		❹ offend
C	ⓥ 사들이다[-드리-]	lay in
B	ⓥ 사라지다	❶ disappear
		❷ die out

		❸melt away
A	ⓝ 사람	man
A	ⓝ 사랑(하)	love
B	ⓐ 사랑스럽다[-따]	(be) lovable
A	ⓥ 사랑하다	love
C	ⓝ 사례(謝禮)(하)[-레]	thanks
C	ⓝ 사립(私立)	private establishment
C	ⓝ 사망(死亡)(하)	death
C	ⓥ 사망하다(死亡-)	die
B	ⓝ 사모님(師母-)	your (good) lady
B	ⓝ 사무(社務)	office work
C	ⓝ 사무소(事務所)	business place
A	ⓝ 사무실(事務室)	office (room)
C	ⓝ 사무직(事務職)	office work
B	ⓝ 사물(事物)	things
C	ⓝ 사방(四方)	four directions
C	ⓝ 사상(思想)	thought
C	ⓝ 사생활(私生活)	private life
C	ⓝ 사설(社說)	editorial
C	ⓐ 사소하다(些少-)	❶(be) trifling

	❷	(be) little
C n	사슴	deer
B n	사실(事實)	fact
B d	사실(史實)	historically
C d	사실상(事實上)[-쌍]	as a matter of fact
A u	사십(四十)	forty
B n	사업(事業)(하)	business
C n	사업가(事業家)[-까]	businessman
C n	사업자(事業者)[-짜]	businessman
B n	사용(使用)(하)	use
B v	사용되다(使用-)	be used
B n	사용자(使用者)	user
A v	사용하다(使用-)	use
B n	사원(社員)	employee
A n	사월(四月)	april
B n	사위	son-in-law
A n	사이	space
C n	사이사이	spaces (between)
B a	사이좋다[-조타]	(be) on good terms
B n	사자(獅子)	lion

210

A ⓝ	사장(社長)	president of a company
C ⓝ	사전(事前)	advance
A ⓝ	사전(辭典)	dictionary
C ⓝ	사정(事情)(하)	❶ situation ❷ solicitation
A ⓝ	사진(寫眞)	photograph
B ⓝ	사진기(寫眞機)	camera
B ⓝ	사촌(四寸)	cousin
C ⓝ	사춘기(思春期)	adolescence
A ⓝ	사탕(沙糖)	candy
C ⓝ	사투리	dialect
C ⓝ	사표(辭表)	(written) resignation
B ⓝ	사회(社會)	society
C ⓝ	사회생활(社會生活)	social life
C ⓝ	사회자(司會者)	MC (master of ceremonies)
B ⓝ	사회적(社會的)	social
C ⓝ	사회주의(社會主義)	socialism
C ⓝ	사회학(社會學)	sociology

B	n 사흘	❶ three days ❷ the third day of the month
A	n 산(山)	mountain
C	n 산길(山-)[-낄]	mountain path
C	n 산부인과(産婦人科)[-꽈]	obstetrics and gynecology
B	n 산소(酸素)	oxygen
B	n 산속(山-)[-쏙]	heart of a mountain
C	n 산업(産業)[사넙]	industry
A	n 산책(散策)(하)	stroll
B	n 살	flesh
A	n 살	years of age
A	v 살다	live
B	v 살리다	❶ rescue ❷ make the most use of ❸ lengthen
C	n 살림(하)	living
C	v 살아가다[사라-]	❶ make one's living

		❷ keep on living
C	v 살아나다[사라-]	❶ revive
		❷ escape (danger)
		❸ flame up again
C	v 살아남다[사라-따]	survive
C	v 살아오다[사라-]	revive
C	n 살인(殺人)(하)[사린]	murder
B	d 살짝	❶ furtively
		❷ softly
B	v 살펴보다	look around
C	v 살피다	observe
C	n 삶[삼]	life
B	v 삶다[삼따]	❶ boil
		❷ bribe
A	u 삼(三)	three
C	v 삼가다	❶ be cautious
		❷ abstain
C	n 삼계탕(蔘鷄湯)[-게-]	chicken broth with ginseng
C	n 삼국(三國)	three countries
C	v 삼다[-따]	make (a thing) of

人

A	ⓤ 삼십(三十)	thirty
A	ⓝ 삼월(三月)[사월]	March
B	ⓝ 삼촌(三寸)	uncle(on the father's side)
C	ⓥ 삼키다	❶ swallow ❷ make (a thing) one's own
C	ⓝ 상(上)	top
C	ⓝ 상(床)	table
C	ⓝ 상(相)	face
B	ⓝ 상(賞)	prize
C	ⓝ 상관(相關)(하)	relation
C	ⓐ 상관없다(相關-)[-과넙따]	(be) unrelated
C	ⓓ 상관없이(相關-)[-과넙씨]	irrespective of
C	ⓝ 상금(賞金)	prize money
C	ⓝ 상담(商談)(하)	business talk
C	ⓝ 상당(相當)(하)	equivalent
C	ⓝ 상당수(相當數)	a good many
C	ⓐ 상당하다(相當-)	(be) proper
C	ⓓ 상당히(相當-)	considerably
B	ⓝ 상대(相對)	❶ facing each

		other
		❷ rival ❸ counter
B	n 상대방(相對方)	counterpart
C	n 상대성(相對性)[-썽]	relativity
C	n 상대적(相對的)	relative
C	n 상대편(相對便)	other party
C	n 상류(上流)[-뉴]	upper stream
C	n 상반기(上半期)	first half of the year
B	n 상상(想像)(하)	imagination
C	n 상상력(想像力)[-녁]	imaginative power
B	v 상상하다(想像-)	imagine
C	n 상식(常識)	common sense
C	n 상업(商業)(하)	commerce
C	n 상인(商人)	merchant
B	n 상자(箱子)	box
C	n 상점(商店)	store
C	n 상징적(象徵的)	symbolical
C	v 상징하다(象徵-)	symbolize
B	n 상처(傷處)	wound
B	n 상추	lettuce

C	ⓐ 상쾌하다(爽快-)	(be) refreshing
C	ⓝ 상태(狀態)	condition
C	ⓝ 상표(商標)	trademark
B	ⓝ 상품(商品)	goods
B	ⓥ 상하다(傷-)	❶injure ❷spoil ❸get thin
C	ⓝ 상황(狀況)	situation
A	ⓡ 새	new
A	ⓝ 새	bird
C	ⓝ 새	interval
C	ⓥ 새기다	carve
B	ⓝ 새끼	youngling
C	ⓥ 새다	leak
B	ⓓ 새로	❶newly ❷for the first time
C	ⓓ 새로이	original figure of newly
C	ⓐ 새롭다[-따]	❶(be) new ❷(be) precious
B	ⓝ 새벽	dawn
B	ⓝ 새소리	sound of birds

B	n 새우	shrimp
C	v 새우다	stay up
B	n 새해	new year
A	n 색(色)	color
A	n 색깔(色-)	color
C	a 색다르다(色-)[-따-]	(be) different
C	n 색연필(色鉛筆)[생년-]	colored pencil
A	n 샌드위치(sandwich)	sandwich
C	n 생	life
A	n 생각(하)	❶ thinking
		❷ intention
		❸ remembrance
B	v 생각나다[-강-]	bring to mind
B	v 생각되다	be supposed
A	v 생각하다[-가카-]	think
B	v 생겨나다	appear
C	n 생기(生氣)	vitality
A	v 생기다	❶ happen
		❷ obtain
		❸ come into being
C	n 생명(生命)	life

C	ⓝ 생물(生物)	living thing
C	ⓝ 생방송(生放送)	live broadcasting
C	ⓝ 생산(生産)(하)	production
C	ⓥ 생산되다(生産-)	output
C	ⓝ 생산력(生産力)[-녁]	production power
C	ⓝ 생산자(生産者)	producer
C	ⓥ 생산하다(生産-)	produce
A	ⓝ 생선(生鮮)	fish
B	ⓝ 생신(生辰)	honorific word of birthday
A	ⓝ 생일(生日)	birthday
A	ⓝ 생활(生活)(하)	living
C	ⓝ 생활비(生活費)	living expenses
C	ⓝ 생활수준(生活水準)	standard of living
C	ⓝ 생활용품(生活用品)[-화룡-]	living necessaries
B	ⓥ 생활하다(生活-)	make a living
B	ⓝ 생활환경(生活環境)	life environment
A	ⓝ 샤워(shower)(하)	shower (bath)
C	ⓝ 서구(西歐)	the West
B	ⓓ 서너	three or four
C	ⓐ 서늘하다	❶ (be) cold

218

		❷ (be) chill
A	v 서다	stand
B	v 서두르다	hurry
B	n 서랍	drawer
B	n 서로	each other
A	d 서로	mutually
B	n 서류(書類)	documents
A	u 서론	thirty
C	n 서명(署名)(하)	signature
C	v 서명하다(署名-)	sign one's name
C	n 서민(庶民)	common people
C	n 서부(西部)	western part
B	n 서비스(service)(하)	service
C	d 서서히(徐徐-)	gradually
B	n 서양(西洋)	the West
C	n 서양인(西洋人)	Westerner
A	n 서울	Seoul
A	n 서울역(-驛)[-력]	Seoul Station
C	n 서적(書籍)	books
A	n 서점(書店)	bookstore
A	n 서쪽(西-)	west

C	n 서클(circle)	❶ circle ❷ association (reading, sports, etc.)
B	a 서투르다	❶ (be) unskilled ❷ (be) strange ❸ (be) clumsy
C	a 서툴다	abbr. of be unskilled
C	n 석	seat
C	u 석	three
C	n 석사(碩士)[-싸]	Master (degree)
B	n 석유(石油)[서규]	petroleum
B	v 섞다[석따]	mix
B	v 섞이다[서끼-]	be mixed
C	n 선(線)	❶ line ❷ cable
C	n 선거(選擧)(하)	election
C	a 선명하다(鮮明-)	(be) distinctive
A	n 선물(膳物)(하)	present
A	v 선물하다(膳物-)	give a present
B	n 선배	senior (of com-

pany, school)
A	n 선생(先生)	teacher
A	n 선생님(先生-)	honorific word of teacher
B	n 선수(選手)	player
C	v 선언하다(宣言)[서넌-]	declare
C	n 선원(船員)[서눤]	crew
C	n 선장(船長)	(ship's) captain
C	n 선전(宣傳)(하)	propaganda
C	v 선정하다(選定-)	select
C	n 선진(先進)	being advanced
C	n 선진국(先進國)	developed country
B	n 선택(選擇)(하)	choice
B	v 선택하다(選擇)[-태카-]	choose
B	n 선풍기(扇風機)	electric fan
C	v 선호하다(選好-)	prefer
B	n 설거지(하)	dishwashing
B	n 설날[-랄]	New Year's Day
C	v 설득하다(說得-)[-뜨카-]	persuade
B	n 설렁탕(-湯)	a kind of beef soup with rice

C	v	설립하다(設立-)[-리파-]	found
A	n	설명(說明)(하)	explanation
C	v	설명되다	be explained
A	v	설명하다(說明-)	explain
C	n	설문(設問)(하)	question
C	d	설사(設使)[-싸]	even if
A	n	설악산(雪嶽山)[서락싼]	Mt.Seorak
C	n	설치(設置)(하)	❶ install ❷ set up
C	v	설치되다(設置)	install
C	v	설치하다(設置-)	install
A	n	설탕(雪糖)	sugar
B	n	섬	island
C	a	섭섭하다[-써파-]	❶ (be) regrettable ❷ (be) vexing
B	n	섭씨(攝氏)	centigrade
C	n	성(城)	castle
B	n	성(姓)	last name
C	n	성(性)	sex
B	n	성격(性格)[-껵]	character
C	n	성경(聖經)	Bible
B	n	성공(成功)(하)	success

C ⓝ	성공적	successful
B ⓥ	성공하다(成功-)	succeed
C ⓝ	성당(聖堂)	Catholic Church
C ⓥ	성립되다(成立)[-닙-]	be made up of
C ⓥ	성립하다(成立-)[-니파-]	be made up of
C ⓝ	성명(聲明)	declaration
B ⓝ	성별(性別)	distinction of sex
C ⓥ	성숙하다(成熟-)[-수카-]	mature
C ⓐ	성실하다(誠實-)	(be) sincere
B ⓝ	성인(成人)	adult
C ⓝ	성장(成長)(하)	growth
C ⓥ	성장하다(成長-)	grow (up)
B ⓝ	성적(成績)	grade
C ⓝ	성적(性的)[-쩍]	sexual
C ⓝ	성질(性質)	❶nature ❷character
B ⓝ	성함(姓銜)	(your, his) esteemed name
A ⓝ	세	year-old
A ⓡ	세	three
C ⓝ	세	generation

B	ⓝ 세계(世界)[-게]	world
C	ⓝ 세계관(世界觀)[-게-]	world view
B	ⓝ 세계적[-게-]	global
B	ⓝ 세금(稅金)	tax
B	ⓝ 세기(世紀)	❶ century ❷ Ages
B	ⓐ 세다	❶ (be) violent ❷ (be) stubborn
C	ⓥ 세다	❶ count ❷ turn gray
C	ⓝ 세대(世代)	❶ generation ❷ people on the same ages
C	ⓐ 세련되다(洗練-)	(be) refined
B	ⓝ 세로	length
C	ⓝ 세미나(seminar)	seminar
B	ⓝ 세상(世上)	❶ world ❷ life
C	ⓔ 세상에(世上-)	on earth
A	ⓝ 세수(洗手)(하)	face washing
B	ⓥ 세우다	❶ stand ❷ park (a car)

		❸ build
		❹ establish (a school)
B	ⓥ 세워지다	be established
C	ⓝ 세월(歲月)	❶ time and tide
		❷ conditions
C	ⓝ 세제(洗劑)	cleaning materials
C	ⓝ 세종대왕(世宗大王)	King Sejong
B	ⓝ 세탁(洗濯)(하)	laundry
A	ⓝ 세탁기(洗濯機)[-끼]	washing machine
B	ⓝ 세탁소(洗濯所)[-쏘]	laundromat
C	ⓝ 세트(set)	❶ set
		❷ (movie) setting
C	ⓐ 섹시하다(sexy-)	(be) sexy
B	ⓝ 센터(center)	❶ center
		❷ center (forward)
A	ⓝ 센티미터(centimeter)	centimeter
C	ⓝ 셈	❶ intention
		❷ calculation

A	ⓤ 셋[섿]	three
A	ⓡ 셋째[섿-]	third
B	ⓝ 소	cattle
B	ⓝ 소개(紹介)(하)	introduction
B	ⓥ 소개되다(紹介-)	introduce
A	ⓥ 소개하다(紹介-)	introduce
C	ⓝ 소규모(小規模)	small scale
C	ⓝ 소극적(消極的)[-쩍]	passive
A	ⓝ 소금	salt
B	ⓝ 소나기	passing rain
B	ⓝ 소나무	pine tree
B	ⓝ 소녀(少女)	girl
B	ⓝ 소년(少年)	boy
C	ⓝ 소득(所得)	income
B	ⓝ 소리	❶ voice ❷ words
B	ⓥ 소리치다	shout
C	ⓝ 소망(所望)(하)	desire
C	ⓝ 소매	sleeve
B	ⓝ 소문(所聞)	rumor
B	ⓥ 소문나다(所聞-)	a rumor get started
C	ⓐ 소박하다(素朴-)[-바카-]	(be) simple

<person's temper>

C	ⓝ 소비(消費)(하)	consumption
B	ⓝ 소비자(消費者)	consumer
C	ⓥ 소비하다(消費-)	spend
B	ⓝ 소설(小說)	novel
B	ⓝ 소설가(小說家)	novelist
C	ⓝ 소속(所屬)(하)	one's position
C	ⓝ 소수(少數)	minority
B	ⓝ 소스(sauce)	sauce
B	ⓝ 소시지(sausage)	sausage
B	ⓝ 소식(消息)	tidings
C	ⓝ 소아과(小兒科)[-꽈]	pediatrics
C	ⓥ 소요되다(所要-)	be needed
C	ⓝ 소용(所用)	usefulness
B	ⓐ 소용없다(所用-)[-업따]	(be) no good
C	ⓝ 소원(所願)(하)	one's desire
C	ⓓ 소위(所謂)	what is called
C	ⓝ 소유(所有)(하)	possession
C	ⓝ 소유자(所有者)	owner
C	ⓥ 소유하다(所有-)	possess
C	ⓝ 소음(騷音)	noise

C	n 소재(素材)	material
B	n 소주(燒酒)	soju (distilled liquor)
C	a 소중하다(所重-)	(be) important
C	d 소중히(所重-)	seriously
C	n 소지품(所持品)	one's belongings
C	n 소질(素質)	temperament
A	n 소파	sofa
B	n 소포(小包)	parcel
A	n 소풍(逍風)	picnic
C	n 소프트웨어(software)	software
C	n 소형(小型)	small size
C	d 소홀히(疏忽-)	carelessly
C	n 소화(消化)(하)	digestion
C	v 소화하다(消化-)	digest
A	n 속	❶ inside ❷ heart ❸ stuffing ❹ real inward feeling
C	n 속담(俗談)[-땀]	proverb
B	n 속도[-또]	speed
C	n 속마음[송-]	one's real intention

C	v 속삭이다[-싸기-]	whisper
C	a 속상하다(-傷-)[-쌍-]	(be) distressing
B	n 속옷[소곧]	underwear
C	v 속이다[소기-]	deceive
B	v 속하다(屬-)[소카-]	belong to
A	n 손	❶ hand
		❷ worker
		❸ helping hand
A	n 손가락[-까-]	finger
C	n 손길[-낄]	one's reach
B	n 손녀(孫女)	granddaughter
A	n 손님	❶ visitor
		❷ passenger
C	n 손등[-뜽]	back of the hand
B	n 손목	wrist
B	n 손바닥[-빠-]	palm of the hand
B	n 손발	❶ limbs
		❷ pace
B	n 손뼉	flat of one's hand
C	d 손수	personally
B	n 손수건(-手巾)[-쑤-]	handkerchief

C	ⓐ 손쉽다[-따]	(be) easy
C	ⓝ 손실(損失)(하)	loss
B	ⓝ 손자(孫子)	grandson
C	ⓥ 손잡다[-따]	❶shake hands
		❷cooperate
B	ⓝ 손잡이[-자비]	knob
C	ⓝ 손질(하)	❶repair
		❷handling
C	ⓥ 손질하다	❶repair
		❷handle
B	ⓝ 손톱	fingernail
C	ⓝ 손해(損害)	damage
B	ⓐ 솔직하다(率直-)[-찌카-]	(be) frank
B	ⓓ 솔직히(率直-)[-찌키]	frankly
C	ⓝ 솜	cotton
C	ⓝ 솜씨	skill
C	ⓥ 솟다[손따]	❶flow out
		❷spring out
		❸blaze up
		❹rise (above)
B	ⓝ 송아지	calf

B	ⓝ 송이	blossom (of a flower)
B	ⓝ 송편(松-)	rice cake steamed on a layer of pine needles
C	ⓝ 쇠	iron
A	ⓝ 쇠고기	beef
B	ⓝ 쇼(show)	show
A	ⓝ 쇼핑(하)(shopping)	shopping
A	ⓝ 수	means
C	ⓝ 수(手)	move (of chess)
C	ⓝ 수(數)	number
A	ⓝ 수건(手巾)	towel
C	ⓝ 수고(하)	pains
B	ⓥ 수고하다	take pains
B	ⓝ 수년(數年)	several years
C	ⓝ 수단(手段)	❶ measure ❷ tool ❸ instrument ❹ skill
C	ⓝ 수도(首都)	capital (city)

C n	수도권(首都圈)[-꿘]	Metropolitan area
C n	수도꼭지(水道-)[-찌]	faucet
B n	수돗물(水道-)[-돈-]	tap water
C n	수동적(受動的)	passive
C v	수리하다(修理-)	repair
C r	수만(數萬)	tens of thousands
B a	수많다(數-)[-만타]	(be) numerous
C n	수면(睡眠)(하)	sleep
C n	수명(壽命)	length of life
A n	수박	watermelon
C r	수백(數百)	hundreds
B n	수상(首相)	prime minister
C n	수석(首席)	top seat
B n	수술(手術)(하)	surgery
C d	수시로(隨時-)	at any time
C r	수십(數十)	several tens
C n	수업(受業)	taking lessons
A n	수업(授業)(하)	teaching lessons
C d	수없이(數-)[-업씨]	innumerably
B n	수염(鬚髯)	beard
A n	수영(水泳)(하)	swimming

A	n 수영장(水泳場)	swimming pool
C	n 수요(需要)	demand
A	n 수요일(水曜日)	Wednesday
B	n 수입(收入)	income
B	n 수입(輸入)(하)	import
C	v 수입되다(輸入-)	import
C	n 수입품(輸入品)	imported goods
B	v 수입하다(輸入-)[-이파-]	import
C	n 수저	spoon
C	n 수준(水準)	standard
C	n 수집(蒐集)(하)	collection
C	v 수집하다(蒐集-)[-지파-]	collect
C	r 수천(數千)	thousands
B	n 수출(輸出)(하)	export
B	v 수출하다(輸出-)	export
C	n 수컷[-컨]	male (animal)
B	n 수표(手票)	check \<a kind of money\>
C	n 수필(隨筆)	miscellaneous writings
B	n 수학(數學)	mathematics

Korean Essential Vocabulary 6000 ❖ 233

B	ⓝ 수학(修學)(하)	learning
C	ⓥ 수행하다(遂行-)	perform
C	ⓝ 수험생(受驗生)	examinee
B	ⓝ 수화기(受話器)	(telephone) receiver
C	ⓝ 숙녀(淑女)[숭-]	lady
B	ⓝ 숙소(宿所)[-쏘]	one's place of abode
B	ⓥ 숙이다[수기-]	lower (one's head)
A	ⓝ 숙제(宿題)(하)[-쩨]	homework
B	ⓝ 순간(瞬間)	moment
C	ⓝ 순간적(瞬間的)	momentary
B	ⓝ 순서(順序)	procedure
C	ⓝ 순수(純粹)(하)	❶ pure ❷ purehearted
B	ⓐ 순수하다(純粹-)	❶ (be) pure ❷ (be) clean and honest
C	ⓝ 순식간(瞬息間)[-깐]	brief instant
C	ⓝ 순위(順位)[수뉘]	ranking
C	ⓐ 순진하다(純眞-)	(be) naive

C	ⓐ 순하다(順-)	❶ (be) tender ❷ (be) well <work> ❸ (be) mild <taste>
A	ⓝ 숟가락[-까-]	spoon
A	ⓝ 술	alcohol
A	ⓝ 술	spoonful
B	ⓝ 술병(-甁)[-뼝]	liquor bottle
B	ⓝ 술자리[-짜-]	drinking party
B	ⓝ 술잔(-盞)[-짠]	liquor glass
B	ⓝ 술집[-찝]	bar
B	ⓝ 숨	❶ breath ❷ crispness of fresh vegetables
C	ⓥ 숨기다	❶ hide away ❷ keep secret
B	ⓥ 숨다[-따]	hide
C	ⓥ 숨지다	breathe one's last
B	ⓝ 숫자(數字)[수짜]	number
B	ⓝ 숲[숩]	forest
A	ⓥ 쉬다	❶ rest ❷ sleep

Korean Essential Vocabulary 6000 ✿ 235

B ⓥ 쉬다	❸ break ❶ spoil <food> ❷ hoarse
A ⓤ 쉰	fifty
A ⓐ 쉽다[-따]	❶ (be) easy ❷ (be) apt to
A ⓝ 슈퍼마켓(supermarket)	supermarket
B ⓝ 스님	❶ master of a Buddhist priest ❷ Buddhist priest
A ⓡ 스무	twenty(use in front of unit)
A ⓤ 스물	twenty
B ⓝ 스스로	by oneself
B ⓓ 스스로	❶ by oneself ❷ voluntarily ❸ of itself
C ⓝ 스승	teacher
B ⓝ 스웨터(sweater)	sweater
C ⓝ 스위치(switch)	switch
C ⓥ 스치다	graze by

B	n 스케이트(skate)	❶ skating
		❷ skates
B	n 스케줄(schedule)	schedule
A	n 스키(ski)	ski
B	n 스키장(ski場)	skiing ground
B	n 스타(star)	❶ celebrity
		❷ slang of general <soldier>
B	n 스타일(style)	style
C	n 스튜디오(studio)	❶ workroom
		❷ movie studio
		❸ TV (radio) studio
A	n 스트레스(stress)	stress
A	n 스포츠(sports)	sport
C	d 슬그머니	furtively
C	d 슬쩍	❶ furtively
		❷ sneakingly
		❸ secretly
B	v 슬퍼하다	feel sad
A	a 슬프다	(be) sad
B	n 슬픔	sorrow

B	n 습관(習慣)[-꽌]	habit
C	n 습기(濕氣)[-끼]	moisture
C	n 승객(乘客)	passenger
C	n 승리(勝利)(하)[-니]	victory
C	v 승리하다(勝利-)[-니-]	win a victory
C	n 승부(勝負)	bout
B	n 승용차(乘用車)	passenger car
C	n 승진(昇進)(하)	promotion
A	n 시(市)	city
A	n 시(時)	o'clock
C	n 시(詩)	poem
C	n 시각(時刻)	time
C	n 시각(視角)	viewpoint
A	n 시간(時間)	❶ time ❷ hour ❸ lesson
A	n 시간(時間)	hour
A	n 시계(時計)	clock
B	n 시골	rural area
C	n 시금치	spinach
C	n 시기(時期)	period

C ⓝ	시기(時機)	(proper) moment
B ⓐ	시끄럽다[-따]	❶(be) noisy
		❷(be) troublesome
C ⓝ	시나리오(scenario)	scenario<movie, TV drama>
B ⓝ	시내(市內)	downtown
B ⓝ	시내버스(市內 bus)	urban bus
B ⓝ	시대(時代)	age
C ⓝ	시대적(時代的)	historical
C ⓝ	시댁(媤宅)	honorific word of husband's house
C ⓝ	시도(試圖)(하)	tryout
B ⓥ	시도하다(試圖-)	try
C ⓥ	시들다	wither
C ⓝ	시디(CD, Compact disc)	CD
C ⓝ	시디롬(CD-ROM)	CD-ROM
B ⓝ	시리즈(series)	❶series
		❷a series of sports
C ⓝ	시멘트(cement)	cement
B ⓝ	시민(市民)	citizen

B	ⓝ 시부모(媤父母)	woman's parents-in-law
C	ⓝ 시선(視線)	one's sight
B	ⓝ 시설(施設)	establishment
C	ⓝ 시스템(system)	❶ channel ❷ regime
B	ⓝ 시아버지(媤-)	woman's father-in-law
C	ⓝ 시야(視野)	visual field
B	ⓝ 시어머니(媤-)	woman's mother-in-law
B	ⓝ 시외(市外)	outskirts
C	ⓝ 시외버스(市外 bus)	cross-country bus
A	ⓐ 시원하다	❶ (be) cool ❷ (be) relieved
A	ⓝ 시월(十月)	October
C	ⓝ 시위(示威)(하)	❶ demonstration ❷ showing one's power
B	ⓝ 시인(詩人)	poet
C	ⓝ 시일(時日)	date and hour

A	ⓝ 시작(始作)(하)	beginning
A	ⓥ 시작되다(始作-)	start
A	ⓥ 시작하다(始作-)[-자카-]	start
A	ⓝ 시장(市場)	market
C	ⓝ 시장(市長)	mayor
B	ⓝ 시절(時節)	time
C	ⓝ 시점(時點)[-쩜]	point of time
C	ⓝ 시중(市中)	in the city
C	ⓝ 시즌(season)	season
B	ⓝ 시집(媤-)	one's husband's home
C	ⓝ 시집(詩集)	collection of poems
C	ⓥ 시집가다(媤-)	woman's being married
B	ⓝ 시청(市廳)	city hall
C	ⓝ 시청률(視聽率)[-뉼]	program rating
B	ⓝ 시청자(視聽者)	TV audience
B	ⓥ 시키다	force
C	ⓝ 시합(試合)(하)	match
A	ⓝ 시험(試驗)(하)	❶ examination

		❷ test <ex. efficiency, strength>
B	n 식	style
B	n 식구(食口)[-꾸]	members of a family
C	n 식기(食器)[-끼]	tablewear
B	v 식다[-따]	get cold <coffee, sweat>
A	n 식당(食堂)[-땅]	restaurant
C	n 식량(食糧)[싱냥]	food
C	n 식료품(食料品)[싱뇨-]	groceries
B	n 식물(植物)[싱-]	plant
B	n 식빵(食-)	baked staple bread with box-shaped mold
A	n 식사(食事)(하)[-싸]	meal
A	v 식사하다(食事-)[-싸-]	take a meal
C	n 식생활(食生活)[-쌩-]	dietary life
C	n 식욕(食慾)[시곡]	appetite
B	n 식용유(食用油)[시굥뉴]	(edible) oil
B	n 식초(食醋)	vinegar

A	n	식탁(食卓)	(dinner) table
B	n	식품(食品)	food
C	n	식품점(食品店)	grocery store
C	v	식히다[시키-]	let cool
B	n	신	excitement
C	n	신(神)	god
C	n	신경(神經)	nerves
B	n	신고(申告)(하)	statement
C	v	신고하다(申告-)	declare (at customs)
C	n	신규(新規)	❶ new regulation ❷ start something new
C	a	신기하다(新奇-)	(be) marvelous
C	n	신념(信念)	belief
A	v	신다[-따]	put on (footwear)
C	n	신라(新羅)[실-]	Shilla (one of ancient nations)
B	n	신랑(新郞)[실-]	bridegroom
A	n	신문(新聞)	newspaper
B	n	신문사(新聞社)	newspaper com-

ㅅ

		pany
B	n 신문지(新聞紙)	newspaper itself
A	n 신발	footwear
B	n 신부(新婦)	bride
C	n 신부(神父)	Catholic priest
C	n 신분(身分)	social position
C	n 신비(神秘)(하)	mystery
C	n 신사(紳士)	gentleman
B	a 신선하다(新鮮-)	(be) fresh
C	n 신설(新設)(하)	new establishment
C	n 신세(身世)	favor
C	n 신세대(新世代)	new generation
C	a 신속하다(迅速-)[-소카-]	(be) quick
B	n 신용(信用)(하)[시농]	trust
C	n 신인(新人)[시닌]	new man
B	n 신입생(新入生)[시닙쌩]	freshman
C	n 신제품(新製品)	new product
C	a 신중하다(愼重-)	(be) prudent
B	n 신청(申請)(하)	application
C	n 신청서(申請書)	application form

C	ⓥ 신청하다(申請-)	apply for
B	ⓝ 신체(身體)	body
C	ⓝ 신체적(身體的)	physical
B	ⓝ 신호(信號)(하)	signal
B	ⓝ 신호등(信號燈)	traffic light
B	ⓝ 신혼부부(新婚夫婦)	newly-married couple
B	ⓝ 신혼여행(新婚旅行)[-녀-]	honeymoon
C	ⓝ 신화(神話)	myth
B	ⓥ 싣다[-따]	❶ load ❷ publish
C	ⓝ 실	thread
C	ⓝ 실감(實感)(하)	actual feeling
B	ⓝ 실내(室內)[-래]	(interior of a) room
B	ⓝ 실력(實力)	one's (real) ability
A	ⓝ 실례(失禮)(하)	discourtesy
A	ⓥ 실례하다(失禮-)	be impolite
C	ⓓ 실로(實-)	really
C	ⓥ 실리다	❶ be reported ❷ get <a thing> loaded

C	n 실망(失望)(하)	disappointment
C	v 실망하다(失望-)	be disappointed
B	n 실수(失手)(하)[-쑤]	mistake
B	v 실수하다(失手-)[-쑤-]	make a mistake
C	n 실습(實習)(하)[-씁]	actual training
C	n 실시(實施)(하)[-씨]	execution
C	v 실시되다(實施-)[-씨-]	be put in operation
C	v 실시하다(實施-)[-씨-]	put in operation
C	d 실은(實-)[시른]	really
C	n 실장(室長)[-짱]	section chief
C	n 실정(實情)[-쩡]	actual circum-stance
C	d 실제(實際)[-쩨]	indeed
B	n 실제(實際)[-쩨]	actuality
C	d 실제로(實際-)[-쩨-]	indeed
C	n 실질적(實質的)[-찔쩍]	substantial
C	n 실천(實踐)(하)	practice
C	v 실천하다(實踐-)	practice
C	n 실체(實體)	substance
C	d 실컷[-컫]	to one's heart's content

C	ⓝ실태(實態)	actual condition
B	ⓝ실패(失敗)(하)	failure
B	ⓥ실패하다(失敗-)	fail
C	ⓝ실험(實驗)(하)	experiment
C	ⓝ실현(實現)(하)	realization
C	ⓥ실현되다(實現-)	be realized
C	ⓥ실현하다(實現-)	realize
A	ⓐ싫다[실타]	(be) unpleasant
B	ⓥ싫어지다[시러-]	disgust
A	ⓥ싫어하다[시러-]	hate
B	ⓐ심각하다(深刻-)[-가카-]	(be) serious
C	ⓥ심각해지다(深刻-)[-가캐-]	get serious
B	ⓥ심다[-따]	plant (a tree)
B	ⓝ심리(心理)[-니]	mental state
C	ⓝ심리적(心理的)[-니-]	psychological
B	ⓝ심부름(하)	errand
C	ⓝ심사(審査)(하)	judgment
C	ⓐ심심하다	❶(be) bored ❷(be) not salty enough
C	ⓝ심장(心臟)	heart

C ⓝ	심정(心情)	one's feeling
C ⓝ	심판(審判)(하)	❶adjudgment
		❷refereeing
B ⓐ	심하다(甚-)	❶(be) extreme
		❷(be) serious
B ⓥ	심해지다(甚-)	get serious
A ⓤ	십(十)	ten
A ⓝ	십이월(十二月)[시비-]	December
A ⓝ	십일월(十一月)[시비뤌]	November
B ⓐ	싱겁다[-따]	(be) not properly salted
C ⓐ	싱싱하다	(be) fresh
A ⓢ	싶다[십따]	❶want
		❷look like
		❸desire
C ⓢ	싶어지다[시퍼-]	want
C ⓝ	싸구려	cheap stuffs
A ⓐ	싸다	❶(be) cheap
		❷(be) well deserved
B ⓥ	싸다	❶wrap up

A	ⓥ 싸우다	❷ surround ❶ fight <enemy> ❷ struggle <difficulty> ❸ quarrel <with a person>
B	ⓝ 싸움(하)	❶ battle ❷ struggle ❸ quarrel
C	ⓓ 싹	bud
C	ⓝ 싼값[-갑]	cheap price
B	ⓝ 쌀	raw rice
C	ⓝ 쌍(雙)	pair
C	ⓝ 쌍둥이(雙-)	twin
B	ⓥ 쌓다[싸타]	❶ lay ❷ build (foundation) ❸ acquire (experience)
B	ⓥ 쌓이다[싸-]	be piled up
C	ⓓ 썩	❶ right away ❷ greatly

B	v 썩다[-따]	❶ spoil
		❷ get rusty
		❸ break <heart>
		❹ live in obscurity
B	v 썰다	slice
C	a 썰렁하다	(be) a bit chilly
B	v 쏘다	❶ shot
		❷ sting <bee>
B	v 쏟다[-따]	❶ pour ❷ flow
		❸ pour out
		❹ concentrate
B	v 쏟아지다[쏘다-]	❶ spout
		❷ gush out
A	v 쓰다	write
A	v 쓰다	use
A	v 쓰다	wear(hat, glasses)
B	a 쓰다	❶ (be) bitter
		❷ (be) disgusted
C	v 쓰다듬다[-따]	❶ touch ❷ stroke
C	v 쓰러지다	❶ fall down
		❷ go bankrupt

A	ⓝ 쓰레기	garbage
B	ⓝ 쓰레기통(-桶)	garbage can
B	ⓥ 쓰이다	be used
C	ⓥ 쓰이다	be written
C	ⓝ 쓴맛[-맏]	bitter taste
C	ⓥ 쓸다	sweep
C	ⓐ 쓸데없다[-떼업따]	(be) useless
C	ⓓ 쓸데없이[-떼업씨]	unnecessarily
C	ⓐ 쓸쓸하다	❶(be) gloomy ❷(be) lonely
C	ⓥ 씌우다[씨-]	❶put (a hat) on (a person's head) ❷cover (a thing) with
B	ⓝ 씨	seed
A	ⓝ 씨(氏)	family name
B	ⓝ 씨름(하)	❶ssireum (folk game) ❷tackling
C	ⓝ 씨앗[-앋]	seed
B	ⓐ 씩씩하다[-씨카-]	(be) brave

Korean Essential Vocabulary 6000

- B Ⅴ 씹다[-따] chew
- C Ⅴ 씻기다[씯끼-] get wet in the rain
- C Ⅴ 씻기다[씯끼-] be washed
- A Ⅴ 씻다[씯따] wash

ㅇ

A	e 아	Ah
B	n 아가씨	❶ young lady
		❷ Miss
A	n 아기	baby
B	n d 아까	some time ago
C	a 아깝다[-따]	❶ (be) pitiful
		❷ (be) wasteful
C	v 아끼다	❶ save
		❷ cherish
B	n 아나운서(announcer)	anchorperson
A	n 아내	wife
C	e 아냐	no
B	e 아뇨	no
A	d 아니	not
B	e 아니	no
A	a 아니다	(be) not
B	e 아니야	no
A	e 아니요	no
C	s 아니하다	be (do) not

C	ⓝ 아드님	your (esteemed) son
A	ⓝ 아들	son
A	ⓝ 아래	❶ bottom ❷ below ❸ under <age, status>
B	ⓝ 아래쪽	lower direction
B	ⓝ 아래층(-層)	lower floor
C	ⓝ 아랫사람[-래싸-]	one's junior
C	ⓝ 아르바이트(독Arbeit)	part-time job
A	ⓐ 아름답다[-따]	❶ (be) pretty ❷ (be) kind-hearted
A	ⓓ 아마	probably
B	ⓓ 아마도	perhaps
A	ⓡ 아무	none
A	ⓞ 아무	anyone
C	ⓞ 아무개	Mr. so and so
B	ⓝ 아무것[-걷]	anything
B	ⓓ 아무래도	anyhow

C	r 아무런	none
B	a 아무렇다[-러타]	(be) unconcerned
B	d 아무리	no matter how
B	d 아무튼	anyway
B	n 아버님	honorific word of father
A	n 아버지	father
A	n 아빠	daddy
C	n 아쉬움	inconvenience (lacking)
C	a 아쉽다[-따]	❶(be) inconvenient ❷(be) pitiful
C	n 아스팔트(asphalt)	asphalt
B	n 아시아(Asia)	Asia
B	e 아아	oh-oh
C	d 아예	from the very first
C	d 아울러	along with
C	e 아유	God
A	n 아이	child

Korean Essential Vocabulary 6000 ✿ 255

B	e	아이	God
A	e	아이고	my goodness
C	n	아이디어(idea)	idea
A	n	아이스크림(ice cream)	ice cream
A	n	아저씨	uncle
A	d	아주	❶ very ❷ forever
A	n	아주머니	❶ aunt ❷ the wife of one's elder brother
A	n	아줌마	auntie
A	d	아직	yet
A	n	아침	morning
A	n	아파트	apartment
A	a	아프다	(be) ill
B	n	아프리카(Africa)	Africa
B	n	아픔	pain
C	e	아하	Aha
A	u	아홉	nine
A	u	아흔	ninety
B	n	악기(樂器)[-끼]	musical instrument

C	n 악몽(惡夢)[앙-]	nightmare
B	n 악수(握手)(하)[-쑤]	handshake
A	d 안	not
C	n 안	❶matter ❷device
A	n 안	❶inside ❷inner room
C	n 안개	fog
A	n 안경(眼鏡)	glasses
C	n 안과(眼科)[-꽈]	ophthalmology
C	v 안기다	fix on (a person)
C	v 안기다	nestle
C	n 안내(案內)(하)	❶guidance ❷notice
B	v 안내하다(案內-)	show
A	e 안녕(安寧)	❶hello ❷bye
A	a 안녕하다(安寧-)	(be) well
A	d 안녕히(安寧-)	peacefully
A	v 안다[-따]	hug
C	n 안동(安東)	Andong
B	a 안되다	❶(be) unsuccessful ❷(be) sorry

A	ⓥ안되다	must not
B	ⓝ안방(-房)[-빵]	main living room
C	ⓝ안부(安否)(하)	welfare
C	ⓥ안심하다(安心-)	be relieved
B	ⓝ안전(安全)	safety
B	ⓐ안전하다(安全-)	(be) safe
C	ⓝ안정(安定)(하)	stability
C	ⓥ안정되다(安定-)	become stabilized
B	ⓝ안주(按酒)	appetizers served with drinks
B	ⓝ안쪽	inside
B	ⓐ안타깝다[-따]	❶(be) nervous ❷(be) frustrating ❸(be) unfortunate
C	ⓝ안팎[안팍]	inside and outside
A	ⓥ앉다[안따]	sit
C	ⓥ앉히다[안치-]	be seated, appoint
A	ⓥ않다[안타]	be not
A	ⓢ않다[안타]	not
B	ⓝ알	spawn, egg

A	ⓥ 알다	❶ know ❷ consider
B	ⓥ 알려지다	come to knowledge
C	ⓝ 알루미늄(aluminium)	aluminium
B	ⓥ 알리다	inform
B	ⓐ 알맞다[-맏따]	(be) proper
C	ⓥ 알아내다[아라-]	find out
B	ⓥ 알아듣다[아라-따]	❶ catch ❷ realize
C	ⓥ 알아보다[아라-]	❶ search ❷ inquire
C	ⓥ 알아주다[아라-]	understand
C	ⓝ 알코올(alcohol)	alcohol
B	ⓥ 앓다[알타]	be ill
B	ⓝ 암(癌)	cancer
C	ⓝ 암시(暗示)(하)	suggestion
C	ⓝ 암컷[-컫]	female (animal)
C	ⓝ 압력(壓力)[암녁]	pressure
A	ⓝ 앞[압]	front
B	ⓝ 앞길[압낄]	way yet to go
C	ⓝ 앞날[암-]	future

C	ⓥ 앞두다[압뚜-]	have ahead
B	ⓝ 앞뒤[압뛰]	before and behind
C	ⓝ 앞문(-門)[암-]	front gate
C	ⓝ 앞바다[압빠-]	offing
C	ⓓ 앞서[압써]	❶ before ❷ in advance
B	ⓥ 앞서다[압써-]	go ahead of
C	ⓥ 앞세우다[압쎄-]	make (a person) go ahead
C	ⓥ 앞장서다[압짱-]	lead
B	ⓝ 앞쪽[압-]	front
B	ⓝ 애	child
C	ⓝ 애	worry
C	ⓥ 애쓰다	strive
B	ⓝ 애인(愛人)	lover
C	ⓝ 애정(愛情)	affection
C	ⓝ 애초(-初)	(very) first
B	ⓝ 액세서리(accessory)	accessory <ring, necklace>
C	ⓝ 액수(額數)[-쑤]	amount

C	n 앨범(album)	album
B	e 야	Hey (you)
C	n 야간(夜間)	night time
A	n 야구(野球)	baseball
C	n 야구장(野球場)	baseball ground
C	n 야단(惹端)(하)	❶ uproar
		❷ scolding
C	d 야옹	meow
B	n 야외(野外)	outskirts (of a town)
B	n 야채(野菜)	vegetable
C	a 야하다(野-)	(be) vulgar
C	n 약	anther
B	r 약(約)	approximately
A	n 약(藥)	medicine
B	n 약간[-깐]	some
B	d 약간[-깐]	somewhat
A	n 약국(藥局)[-꾹]	drugstore
A	n 약속(約束)(하)[-쏙]	promise
A	v 약속하다(約束-)[-쏘카-]	promise
C	n 약수(藥水)[-쑤]	mineral water

C ⓝ	약점(弱點)[-쩜]	weak point
C ⓝ	약품(藥品)	medicines
B ⓐ	약하다(弱-)[야카-]	(be) weak
C ⓥ	약해지다(弱-)[야캐-]	get weak
C ⓝ	약혼녀(約婚女)[야콘-]	fiancée
C ⓝ	약혼자(約婚者)[야콘-]	fiancé
C ⓐ	얄밉다[-따]	(be) mean and nasty
B ⓐ	얇다[얄따]	(be) thin
C ⓡ	양(兩)	two
C ⓝ	양(孃)	Miss
C ⓝ	양(羊)	sheep
B ⓝ	양(量)	quantity
C ⓝ	양국(兩國)	two countries
B ⓝ	양념	dressing materials (seasoning)
C ⓝ	양력(陽曆)[-녁]	solar calendar
A ⓝ	양말(洋襪)	socks
B ⓝ	양배추(洋-)	cabbage
C ⓝ	양보(讓步)(하)	concession
B ⓥ	양보하다(讓步-)	yield

A	n	양복(洋服)	suit
C	n	양상추(洋-)	lettuce
C	n	양식(樣式)	❶ pattern
			❷ social rules
C	n	양식(洋食)	Western food
C	n	양심(良心)	conscience
C	n	양옆(兩-)[-엽]	both sides
C	n	양주(洋酒)	Western liquors
B	n	양쪽(兩-)	both sides
B	n	양파(洋-)	onion
B	a	얕다[얃따]	(be) shallow
C	e	얘	there
A	n	얘기(하)	conversation
A	v	얘기하다	chatter
A	e	어	yeap
C	v	어기다	violate
A	n	어깨	shoulder
A	r	어느	which
C	d	어느덧[-덛]	before one knows
B	d	어느새	❶ so soon

		❷ already
B	ⓥ 어두워지다	get dark
B	ⓝ 어둠	darkness
B	ⓐ 어둡다[-따]	❶ (be) dark
		❷ (be) weak <sight>
A	ⓞ 어디	where
A	ⓔ 어디	where
A	ⓐ 어떠하다	(be) how
A	ⓡ 어떤	❶ whom
		❷ some of
A	ⓐ 어떻다[-떠타]	(be) how
B	ⓝ 어려움	difficulty
C	ⓥ 어려워지다	get difficult
A	ⓐ 어렵다[-따]	(be) difficult
A	ⓝ 어른	adult
B	ⓐ 어리다	(be) very young
B	ⓥ 어리다	gather in the eyes(tears)
C	ⓐ 어리석다[-따]	(be) foolish
B	ⓝ 어린아이[-리나-]	child

264

B n	어린애[-리내]	abbr. of child
A n	어린이[-리니]	child
B n	어린이날[-리니-]	Children's Day
B e	어머	why
A n	어머니	mother
B n	어머님	(my) dear mother
B a	어색하다(語塞-)[-새카-]	(be) awkward
A d	어서	in haste
B v	어울리다	match
C n	어저께	yesterday
A n d	어제	yesterday
B n	어젯밤[-제빰]	last night
C a	어지럽다[-따]	(be) dizzy
C d	어쨌든[-짿뜬]	anyway
C d	어쩌다	❶ by chance
		❷ scarcely
B v	어쩌다	how
C d	어쩌다가	❶ by chance
		❷ scarcely
B d	어쩌면	maybe
B d	어쩐지	without knowing

		why
C	ⓓ 어쩜	how
C	ⓓ 어찌	maybe
C	ⓓ 어찌나	too
C	ⓥ 어찌하다	be indisputable
B	ⓤ 억(億)	hundred million
C	ⓐ 억울하다(抑鬱-)[어굴-]	feel victimized
A	ⓝ 언니	elder sister
C	ⓝ 언덕	hill
C	ⓝ 언론(言論)[얼-]	speech
C	ⓝ 언어(言語)[어너]	language
A	ⓐⓓ 언제	when
A	ⓓ 언제나	always
B	ⓓ 언젠가	someday
B	ⓥ 얹다[언따]	place (something) on
B	ⓥ 얻다[-따]	get
C	ⓥ 얻어먹다[어더-따]	❶ get treated to ❷ beg
A	ⓝ 얼굴	face
B	ⓥ 얼다	freeze

B	d 얼른	fast
C	v 얼리다	to be freezing
A	n 얼마	somewhat
C	n 얼마간(-間)	some
A	d 얼마나	❶ how much ❷ how
B	n 얼음[어름]	ice
C	d 얼핏[-핃]	a glimpse of
C	a 엄격하다(嚴格-)[-껴카-]	(be) stern
A	n 엄마	mommy
C	a 엄숙하다(嚴肅-)[-수카-]	(be) solemn
C	a 엄청나다	(be) absurd
C	v 업다[-따]	carry (someone) on one's back
B	n 업무(業務)[엄무]	affairs
C	n 업종(業種)[-쫑]	category of business
C	n 업체(業體)	(business) enterprise
A	a 없다[업따]	(be) lacking
B	v 없애다[업쌔-]	❶ abolish

		❷ exterminate
B	ⓥ 없어지다[업써-]	disappear
B	ⓓ 없이[업씨]	without
C	ⓥ 엇갈리다[얻깔-]	cross (each other)
C	ⓝ 엉덩이	hips
B	ⓐ 엉뚱하다	❶ (be) extravagant
		❷ (be) unexpected
C	ⓝ 엉망	mess
C	ⓝ 엉터리	fake
B	ⓓ 엊그제[얻끄-]	a few days ago
C	ⓥ 엎드리다[업뜨-]	lie on one's face
C	ⓔ 에	uh
B	ⓝ 에너지(energy)	❶ energy
		❷ vitality
A	ⓝ 에어컨	air conditioner
B	ⓝ 엔(일en)	yen \<currency unit of Japan\>
C	ⓝ 엔진(engine)	engine
B	ⓝ 엘리베이터(elevator)	elevator
B	ⓝ 여(女)	abbr. of woman
C	ⓝ 여가(餘暇)	leisure

C d	여간(如干)	ordinarily
C n	여건(與件)[-껀]	given condition
C v	여겨지다	be regarded
B n	여고생(女高生)	high school girl
B n	여관(旅館)	inn
C n	여군(女軍)	woman soldier
A n	여권(旅券)[-꿘]	passport
A o	여기	here
C v	여기다	regard
B n	여기저기	here and there
B n	여대생(女大生)	college woman
A u	여덟[-덜]	eight
A n	여동생(女同生)	younger sister
A u	여든	eighty
A r	여러	many
A o	여러분	ladies and gentlemen
C n	여럿[-럳]	many (people)
C n	여론(輿論)	public opinion
A n	여름	summer
B n	여름철	summertime

B	e 여보	low talk of hello
A	e 여보세요	hello
A	u 여섯[-섣]	six
B	n 여성(女性)	woman
C	n 여왕(女王)	queen
B	n 여우	fox
B	n 여유(餘裕)	calmness
C	n 여인(女人)	woman
A	n 여자(女子)	lady
C	a 여전하다(如前-)	(be) unchanged
C	d 여전히(如前-)	as ever
B	n 여직원(女職員)[-지권]	woman worker
B	v 여쭈다	ask(to one's elders)
A	n 여학생(女學生)[-쌩]	girl student
A	n 여행(旅行)(하)	travel
B	n 여행사	travel agency
A	v 여행하다(旅行-)	travel
C	n 역(役)	role(of play or movie)
A	n 역(驛)	station

A	n 역사(歷史)[-싸]	history
B	n 역사가(歷史家))[-싸-]	historian
C	n 역사상(歷史上)[-싸-]	in history
B	n 역사적(歷史的)[-싸-]	historical
C	n 역사학(歷史學)[-싸-]	historical science
B	d 역시(亦是)[-씨]	as well
B	n 역할(役割)(하)[여칼]	role
C	n 연간(年間)	for a year
C	n 연결(連結)(하)	connection
B	v 연결되다(連結)	connect
C	n 연관(聯關)(하)	relation
B	n 연구(研究)(하)	research
B	n 연구소(研究所)	research institute
C	n 연구실(研究室)	laboratory
C	n 연구원(研究員)	research worker
B	n 연구자(研究者)	researcher
B	v 연구하다(研究-)	research
C	n 연극(演劇)(하)	drama
B	n 연기(煙氣)	smoke
C	n 연기(延期)(하)	delay
B	n 연기(演技)(하)	acting

C	v	연기되다(延期-)	be delayed
C	n	연기자(演技者)	performer
C	v	연기하다(延期-)	delay
C	n	연두색(軟豆色)	yellowish green color
C	n	연락(連絡)(하)[열-]	contact
B	n	연락처(連絡處)[열-]	contact address
B	v	연락하다(連絡-)[열라카-]	contact
C	n	연령(年齡)[열-]	age
B	n	연말(年末)	year-end
C	v	연상하다(聯想-)	associate
C	n	연설(演說)(하)	speech
B	n	연세(年歲)	honorific word of age
C	n	연속(連續)(하)	continuity
A	n	연습(練習)(하)	training
A	v	연습하다(練習-)[-스파-]	practice
C	n	연애(戀愛)(하)[여내]	love
C	n	연예인(演藝人)[여녜-]	entertainer
C	n	연인(戀人)[여닌]	lover
C	n	연장(延長)(하)	extension

C	n	연주(演奏)(하)	(musical) performance
C	n	연출(演出)(하)	production
C	v	연출하다(演出-)	direct
A	n	연필(鉛筆)	pencil
B	a	연하다(軟-)	(be) soft
C	n	연합(聯合)(하)	combination
B	n	연휴(連休)	holidays in a row
A	u	열	ten
B	n	열(熱)	heat
C	n	열기(熱氣)	excitement
A	v	열다	open
B	v	열리다	bear (fruit)
B	v	열리다	be opened
C	n	열매	fruit
A	n	열쇠[-쐬]	key
A	d	열심히(熱心-)[-씸-]	hard
C	n	열정(熱情)[-쩡]	passion
C	v	열중하다(熱中-)[-쭝-]	devote oneself
B	n	열차(列車)	train
B	n	열흘	ten days

C ⓐ	얇다[열따]	(be) thin
C ⓝ	염려(念慮)(하)[-녀]	concern
B ⓥ	염려하다(念慮-)[-녀-]	worry
B ⓝ	엽서(葉書)[-써]	postcard
C ⓥ	엿보다[엳뽀-]	steal a glance
C ⓓ	영(永)	forever
A ⓝ	영국(英國)	England
C ⓝ	영남(嶺南)	southeastern part of Korea
C ⓝ	영상(映像)	image
B ⓝ	영상(零上)	above zero
C ⓝ	영양(營養)	nutrition
A ⓝ	영어(英語)	English language
C ⓝ	영업(營業)(하)	sales
C ⓝ	영역(領域)	sphere
C ⓝ	영웅(英雄)	hero
B ⓐ	영원하다(永遠-)	(be) eternal
B ⓓ	영원히(永遠-)	forever
B ⓝ	영하(零下)	below zero
C ⓝ	영향(影響)	influence
C ⓝ	영향력(影響力)[-녁]	influencing

		power
C n	영혼(靈魂)	soul
A n	영화(映畫)	movie
C n	영화관(映畫館)	movie theater
C n	영화배우(映畫俳優)	movie actor
C n	영화제(映畫祭)	film festival
A n	옆[엽]	side
C n	옆구리[엽꾸-]	flank
B n	옆방(-房)[엽빵]	next room
B n	옆집[엽찝]	next house
C n	예	old days
A e	예	yes
B n	예(例)	example
C n	예감(豫感)(하)	presentiment
C v	예고하다(豫告-)	give (advance) notice
B n	예금(預金)(하)	deposit
B v	예매하다(豫買-)	buy in advance
C n	예방(豫防)(하)	prevention
C v	예방하다(豫防-)	prevent
C n	예보(豫報)(하)	forecast

C	n 예비(豫備)(하)	preparation
A	a 예쁘다	(be) pretty
C	n 예산(豫算)(하)	budget
B	n 예상(豫想)(하)	expectation
C	v 예상되다(豫想-)	be expected
C	v 예상하다(豫想-)	expect
C	n 예선(豫選)(하)	preliminary match
A	u 예순	sixty
B	n 예술(藝術)	art
B	n 예술가(藝術家)	artist
C	n 예술적(藝術的)[-쩍]	artistic
C	n 예습(豫習)(하)	preparations (of one's lessons)
C	v 예습하다(豫習-)[-스파-]	prepare lessons
C	n 예식장(禮式場)[-짱]	marriage ceremony hall
B	n 예약(豫約)(하)	reservation
C	v 예약하다(豫約-)[-야카-]	make a reservation
C	n 예외(例外)	exception
C	n 예의(禮儀)[-이]	etiquette

B	n 예전	old days
B	n 예절(禮節)	manners
B	n 예정(豫定)(하)	previous arrangement
C	v 예정되다(豫定-)	arrange beforehand
C	v 예측하다(豫測-)[-츠카-]	predict
C	d 예컨대(例-)	such as
B	r 옛[엳]	ancient
A	n 옛날[엔-]	old days
B	n 옛날이야기[엔-]	old story
B	e 오	o, dear
A	u 오(五)	five
B	v 오가다	come and go
A	nd 오늘	today
B	n 오늘날[-랄]	these days
A	s 오다	…ing
A	v 오다	come
C	n 오락(娛樂)(하)	entertainment
A	d 오래	for a long time
A	n 오래간만	after a long time

B ⓓ 오래도록	for a long time
B ⓥ 오래되다	for a long time
B ⓝ 오래전(-前)	long time ago
B ⓡ 오랜	long
A ⓝ 오랜만	after a long time
B ⓝ 오랫동안[-래똥-]	for a long time
A ⓝ 오렌지(orange)	orange
C ⓓ 오로지	only
C ⓥ 오르내리다	rise and fall
A ⓥ 오르다	❶ go up ❷ climb (mountain)
B ⓝ 오른발	right foot
B ⓝ 오른손	right hand
A ⓝ 오른쪽	right side
B ⓝ 오리	duck
B ⓝ 오븐(oven)	oven
A ⓝ 오빠	girl's elder brother
A ⓤ 오십(五十)	fifty
C ⓝ 오염(汚染)	pollution
C ⓥ 오염되다(汚染-)	be polluted

A	ⓝ 오월(五月)	May
B	ⓝ 오이	cucumber
A	ⓝ 오전(午前)	forenoon
B	ⓓ 오직	merely
B	ⓝ 오징어	squid
C	ⓝ 오페라(opera)	opera
B	ⓝ 오피스텔(office+hotel)	studio apartment
C	ⓝ 오해(誤解)(하)	misunderstanding
A	ⓝ 오후(午後)	afternoon
C	ⓓ 오히려	rather (than)
C	ⓝ 옥상(屋上)[-쌍]	rooftop
B	ⓝ 옥수수[-쑤-]	corn
B	ⓡ 온	whole
C	ⓡ 온갖[-갇]	all kinds of
B	ⓝ 온도(溫度)	temperature
C	ⓝ 온돌(溫乭)	Korean under-floor heating (system)
C	ⓝ 온라인(on-line)	on-line
B	ⓝ 온몸	whole body
C	ⓝ 온종일(-終日)	all day (long)

B	d	온통	wholly
C	r	올	this year
C	n	올	ply
C	n	올가을[-까-]	this autumn
A	v	올라가다	go up
C	v	올라서다	step up
B	v	올라오다	come up
C	v	올라타다	❶ride ❷jump on
B	v	올려놓다[-노타]	put (something) up on
C	v	올려다보다	look up
C	v	올리다	raise
B	n	올림픽(Olympic)	Olympics
C	a	올바르다	(be) upright
C	n	올여름[-려-]	this summer
A	n	올해	this year
B	v	옮기다[옴-]	❶move ❷transfer
B	a	옳다[올타]	(be) rightful
A	n	옷[옫]	clothes
C	n	옷차림[옫-]	one's (personal)

		appearance
B	e 와	wow
C	n 와이셔츠(white shirts)	dress shirt
B	n 와인(wine)	wine
B	a 완벽하다(完璧-)[-벼카-]	(be) perfect
C	n 완성(完成)(하)	completion
C	v 완성되다(完成-)	be completed
C	v 완성하다(完成-)	complete
C	n 완전(完全)	perfection
C	a 완전하다(完全-)	(be) complete
B	d 완전히(完全-)	perfectly
B	n 왕(王)	king
C	n 왕비(王妃)	queen
C	n 왕자(王子)	prince
A	d 왜	why
A	d 왜냐하면	because
B	d 왠지	for some reason
B	n 외(外)	out
C	n 외갓집(外家-)[-가찝]	one's mother's maiden home
C	n 외과(外科)[-꽈]	(science of) sur-

		gery
B	n 외교(外交)(하)	diplomacy
B	n 외교관(外交官)	diplomat
A	n 외국(外國)	foreign country
A	n 외국어(外國語)[-구거]	foreign language
A	n 외국인(外國人)[-구긴]	foreigner
C	v 외다	learn by heart
C	n 외로움	loneliness
B	a 외롭다[-따]	(be) lonely
C	v 외면하다(外面-)	look away
C	n 외모(外貌)	external features
C	n 외부(外部)	outside
B	n 외삼촌(外三寸)	uncle on one's mother's side
C	n 외아들	only son
B	v 외우다	learn by heart
C	n 외제(外製)	foreign-made
B	n 외출(外出)(하)	outing
B	v 외출하다(外出-)	go out
C	v 외치다	shout
C	n 외침	shout

B	n 외할머니(外-)	mother of one's mother
C	n 외할아버지(外-)[-하라-]	father of one's mother
B	n 왼발	left foot
B	n 왼손	left hand
A	n 왼쪽	left side
C	r 요	this
C	n 요구(要求)(하)	demand
C	v 요구되다(要求-)	demand
B	v 요구하다(要求-)	demand
B	n 요금(料金)	fare
A	n 요리(料理)(하)	cooking
C	n 요리사(料理師)	cook
A	v 요리하다(料理-)	cook
B	n 요새	recently
C	v 요약하다(要約-)[-야카-]	summary
A	n 요일(曜日)	day of the week
A	n 요즈음	these days
A	n 요즘	these days
B	n 요청(要請)(하)	request

C	v 요청하다(要請-)	request
C	n 욕(辱)(하)	abuse
B	n 욕실(浴室)[-씰]	bathroom
B	n 욕심(欲心)[-씸]	greed
C	v 욕하다(辱-)[요카-]	speak ill of
C	n 용(龍)	dragon
C	a 용감하다(勇敢-)	(be) brave
C	n 용기(勇氣)	courage
C	n 용기(容器)	container
C	n 용도(用途)	use
B	n 용돈(用-)[-똔]	pocket money
C	n 용서(容恕)(하)	forgiveness
C	v 용서하다(容恕-)	forgive
C	n 용어(用語)	term(word)
C	n 우려(憂慮)(하)	concern
A	o 우리	we
A	n 우리나라	one's (own) country
B	n 우리말	one's mother tongue
A	n 우산(雨傘)	umbrella

284

B d	우선(于先)	first of all
B a	우수하다(優秀-)	(be) superior
C a	우습다[-따]	(be) funny
B n	우승(優勝)(하)	championship
B v	우승하다(優勝-)	win the victory
C a	우아하다(優雅-)	(be) elegant
B d	우연히(偶然-)	accidentally
B a	우울하다(憂鬱-)	(be) gloomy
A n	우유(牛乳)	milk
C n	우정(友情)	friendship
C n	우주(宇宙)	universe
A n	우체국(郵遞局)	post office
C n	우편(郵便)	post
B n	우표(郵票)	(postage) stamp
B n	운(運)	luck
A n	운동(運動)(하)	exercise
B n	운동복(運動服)	sportswear
A n	운동장(運動場)	playground
A v	운동하다(運動-)	take exercise
A n	운동화(運動靴)	sports shoes
C n	운명(運命)	fate

C	n 운반(運搬)(하)	transportation
C	v 운영하다(運營-)[우녕-]	operate
A	n 운전(運轉)(하)	driving
B	n 운전기사(運轉技士)	driver(job)
C	n 운전사(運轉士)	driver(job)
B	n 운전자(運轉者)	driver
A	v 운전하다(運轉-)	drive
C	n 운행(運行)(하)	operation
A	v 울다	cry
C	v 울리다	make someone cry
B	v 울리다	ring
B	n 울산(蔚山)[-싼]	Ulsan
B	n 울음[우름]	crying
C	n 울음소리[우름쏘-]	cry
B	v 움직이다[-지기-]	move
C	n 움직임[-지김]	movement
B	v 웃기다[욷끼-]	amuse
A	v 웃다[욷따]	laugh
B	n 웃어른[우더-]	one's elders
B	n 웃음[우슴]	laugh

C [n]	웃음소리[우슴쏘-]	laughter
C [d]	워낙	❶ overly
		❷ originally
A [n]	원	won
C [e]	원	gosh
C [n]	원(圓)	circle
C [n]	원고(原稿)	manuscript
B [n]	원래(元來)[월-]	originally
C [n]	원서(願書)	written application
B [n]	원숭이	monkey
C [n]	원인(原因)[워닌]	cause
C [n]	원장(院長)	director (of a hospital or academy)
B [n]	원피스(one-piece)	one-piece (dress)
B [v]	원하다(願-)	want
A [n]	월(月)	month
B [n]	월급(月給)	(monthly) salary
B [n]	월드컵(World Cup)	World Cup
C [n]	월세(月貰)[-쎄]	monthly rent
A [n]	월요일(月曜日)[워료-]	Monday
B [n]	웨이터(waiter)	waiter

C	r 웬	what
C	a 웬만하다	(be) tolerable
B	n 웬일[-닐]	what matter
A	n 위	upper part
C	n 위(位)	rank
C	n 위(胃)	stomach
C	n 위기(危機)	crisis
C	a 위대하다(偉大-)	(be) great
C	n 위로(慰勞)(하)	consolation
C	v 위로하다(慰勞-)	console
B	n 위반(違反)(하)	violation
C	v 위반하다(違反-)	violate
C	n 위법(違法)(하)	illegality
C	n 위성(衛星)	satellite
B	n 위아래	up and down
C	n 위원(委員)	committee member
C	n 위원장(委員長)	chairperson
C	n 위주(爲主)	giving the first consideration
B	n 위쪽	upper direction

B	n 위층(-層)	upper floor
B	n 위치(位置)(하)	location
B	v 위치하다(位置-)	be located
B	v 위하다(爲-)	do for the sake
A	n 위험(危險)(하)	danger
C	n 위험성(危險性)[-썽]	dangerousness
A	a 위험하다(危險-)	(be) dangerous
C	n 위협(威脅)(하)	threat
C	n 윗몸[윈-]	upper part of the body
C	n 윗사람[위싸-]	one's senior
B	n 유교(儒敎)	confucianism
B	d 유난히	conspicuously
C	a 유능하다(有能-)	(be) capable
B	n 유럽(Europe)	Europe
B	n 유리(琉璃)	glass
B	n 유리창(琉璃窓)	glass window
C	a 유리하다(有利-)	(be) profitable
C	n 유머	humor
B	n 유명(有名)	famousness
A	a 유명하다(有名-)	(be) famous

C	n 유물(遺物)	remains
C	v 유발하다(誘發-)	❶induce
		❷lead to
C	a 유사하다(類似-)	(be) similar
C	n 유산(遺産)	inheritance
A	n 유월(六月)	June
C	v 유의하다(留意-)	pay attention to
C	n 유적(遺跡)	ruins
C	n 유적지(遺跡地)[-찌]	historic site
C	v 유지되다(維持-)	maintain
C	v 유지하다(維持-)	maintain
B	n 유치원(幼稚園)	kindergarten
B	n 유학(儒學)	Confucianism
B	n 유학(留學)(하)	studying abroad
B	n 유학생(留學生)[-쌩]	student studying abroad
B	n 유행(流行)(하)	vogue
B	v 유행하다(流行-)	be in vogue
C	n 유형(類型)	pattern
A	u 육(六)	six
C	n 육군(陸軍)[-꾼]	army

C n	육상(陸上)[-쌍]	(on the) ground
A u	육십(六十)[-씹]	sixty
C n	육체(肉體)	body
C n	육체적(肉體的)	bodily
C d	으레	necessarily
B e	으응	oh
C n	은(銀)	silver
C a	은은하다(隱隱-)[으는-]	(be) roaring
A n	은행(銀行)	bank
C n	은행나무(銀杏-)	ginkgo
B e	음	well
C n	음력(陰曆)[-녁]	lunar calendar
B n	음료(飲料)[-뇨]	beverage
B n	음료수(飲料水)[-뇨-]	drinking water
C n	음반(音盤)	phonograph record
C n	음성(音聲)	voice
A n	음식(飲食)	food (and drink)
C n	음식물(飲食物)[-싱-]	food (and drink)
C n	음식점(飲食店)[-쩜]	restaurant
A n	음악(音樂)[으막]	music

B	ⓝ 음악가(音樂家)[으막까]	musician
C	ⓝ 음주(飮酒)(하)	drinking
B	ⓔ 응	oh
C	ⓥ 응답하다(應答-)[-다파-]	respond
B	ⓝ 의견(意見)	opinion
C	ⓝ 의논(議論)(하)	consultation
C	ⓥ 의논하다(議論-)	consult
C	ⓝ 의도(意圖)(하)	intention
C	ⓝ 의도적(意圖的)	knowing
C	ⓝ 의류(衣類)	clothes
C	ⓝ 의무(義務)	duty
C	ⓝ 의문(疑問)(하)	question
B	ⓝ 의미(意味)(하)	meaning
B	ⓥ 의미하다(意味-)	mean
C	ⓝ 의복(衣服)	clothes
C	ⓝ 의사(意思)	intention
A	ⓝ 의사(醫師)	doctor
C	ⓝ 의식(儀式)	ceremony
C	ⓝ 의식(意識)(하)	one's senses
C	ⓥ 의식하다(意識-)[-시카-]	be conscious of
C	ⓝ 의심(疑心)(하)	suspicion

B Ⓥ	의심하다(疑心-)	doubt
C ⓓ	의외로(意外-)	unexpectedly
C ⓝ	의욕(意欲)	will
C ⓝ	의원(議員)	assemblyman
A ⓝ	의자(椅子)	chair
C Ⓥ	의존하다(依存-)	depend on
C ⓝ	의지(意志)	will
C Ⓥ	의지하다(依支-)	lean on
B Ⓥ	의하다(依-)	depend on
C ⓝ	의학(醫學)	medical science
C ⓝ	이	this
A ⓝ	이	tooth
A ⓞ	이	this
A ⓡ	이	person
A ⓤ	이(二)	two
C ⓓ	이같이[-가치]	like this
A ⓞ	이거	this
A ⓞ	이것[-걷]	this thing
B ⓝ	이것저것[-걷쩌걷]	this and that
A ⓞ	이곳[-곧]	here
B ⓝ	이곳저곳[-곧쩌곧]	here and there

B	ⓥ 이기다	❶ win
		❷ overcome
C	ⓥ 이끌다	❶ pull ❷ lead
B	ⓝ 이날	this day
C	ⓓ 이내	soon
C	ⓝ 이내	within
C	ⓝ 이념	ideology
C	ⓞ 이놈	this guy
C	ⓝ 이다음	next
C	ⓝ 이달	this month
C	ⓓ 이대로	as it is
C	ⓝ 이데올로기(독Ideologie)	ideology
B	ⓝ 이동(移動)(하)	movement
C	ⓥ 이동하다(移動-)	move
B	ⓓ 이따가	after a while
C	ⓓ 이따금	from time to time
A	ⓝ 이때	at this time
C	ⓝ 이래(以來)	after that
C	ⓥ 이러다	do like this
B	ⓐ 이러하다	(be) like this
A	ⓡ 이런	such

C ⓡ	이런저런	something or another
B ⓓ	이렇게[-러케]	like this
A ⓐ	이렇다[-러타]	(be) like this
C ⓝ	이력서(履歷書)[-써]	resume
C ⓝ	이론적(理論的)	theoretical
C ⓐ	이롭다(利-)[-따]	(be) beneficial
B ⓥ	이루다	❶ realize ❷ achieve
B ⓥ	이루어지다	❶ get accomplished ❷ be formed
C ⓥ	이룩하다[-루카-]	establish
B ⓥ	이뤄지다	❶ get accomplished ❷ be formed
C ⓥ	이르다	inform
B ⓐ	이르다	(be) early
B ⓥ	이르다	❶ extend to ❷ reach
A ⓝ	이름	name

B d	이리	this way
C d	이리저리	in places
B n	이마	forehead
B n	이모(姨母)	one's mother's sister
B d	이미	already
B n	이미지(image)	image
C n	이민(移民)(하)	emigration
B n	이발소(理髮所)[-쏘]	barbershop
A n	이번(-番)	this time
C n	이별(離別)(하)	parting
A o	이분	this gentleman
B n	이불	bedclothes
B n	이빨	tooth
B n	이사(移徙)(하)	move
C n	이사장(理事長)	chief director
B v	이사하다(移徙-)	change one's residence
B n	이상(理想)	goal (of ambition)
B n	이상(以上)	more than
B n	이상(異常)	strangeness

C	n	이상적(理想的)	ideal
C	a	이상하다(異常-)	(be) strange
B	n	이성(理性)	rationality
C	n	이성(異性)	other sex
C	n	이슬	dew
A	u	이십(二十)	twenty
A	n	이야기(하)	❶ old story
			❷ conversation
A	v	이야기하다	❶ tell a story
			❷ speak
C	d	이어	subsequently
C	d	이어서	subsequently
C	v	이어지다	be linked
B	n	이외(以外)	except
B	n	이용(利用)(하)	utilization
B	v	이용되다(利用-)	use
C	n	이용자(利用者)	user
B	v	이용하다(利用-)	use
B	n	이웃(하)[-욷]	❶ vicinity
			❷ neighbor
B	n	이웃집[-욷찝]	neighbor's house

A	n 이월(二月)	February
B	n 이유(理由)	reason
C	d 이윽고[-꼬]	❶ after a while ❷ soon after
B	n 이익(利益)	profit
C	n 이자(利子)	interest <bank>
B	n 이전(以前)	former times
A	d 이제	now
A	n 이제	now
C	d 이제야	now
C	n 이중(二重)	duplication
A	o 이쪽	this side
B	n 이튿날[-튼-]	next day
B	n 이틀	two days
B	n 이하(以下)	less than
C	n 이해(利害)	gain and loss
B	n 이해(理解)(하)	understanding
C	n 이해관계(利害關係)[-게]	interest
C	v 이해되다(理解-)	understand
A	v 이해하다(理解-)	understand
B	n 이혼(離婚)(하)	divorce

B	v 이혼하다(離婚-)	divorce
B	n 이후(以後)	after this
C	a 익다[-따]	(be) familiar
B	v 익다[-따]	ripe
B	a 익숙하다[-쑤카-]	(be) familiar
B	v 익숙해지다[-쑤캐-]	get skillful
C	v 익히다[이키-]	boil
C	v 익히다[이키-]	practice
C	n 인	man
B	n 인간(人間)	❶ man ❷ human beings
C	n 인간관계(人間關係)[-게]	human relations
C	n 인간성(人間性)[-썽]	❶ human nature ❷ character
C	n 인간적(人間的)	humane
C	n 인격(人格)[-격]	❶ personality ❷ dignity
C	n 인공(人工)	❶ artificial ❷ human work
B	n 인구(人口)	population
C	n 인근(隣近)	vicinity

Korean Essential Vocabulary 6000 ❃ 299

B	n	인기(人氣)[-끼]	popularity
C	n	인도	sidewalk
C	n	인류(人類)[일-]	human beings
C	n	인물(人物)	person
B	n	인분(人分)	portion(food quantity for each person)
C	n	인사(人事)	personal affairs
A	n	인사(人士)	personage
A	n	인사(人事)(하)	greetings
B	n	인사말(人事-)	compliments
A	v	인사하다(人事-)	greet
B	n	인삼(人蔘)	ginseng
B	n	인삼차(人蔘茶)	ginseng tea
B	n	인상(人相)	personal appearance
B	n	인상(印象)	impression
C	n	인상(引上)(하)	❶ pulling up ❷ raising
C	n	인상적(印象的)	impressive
B	n	인생(人生)	human life

C	n 인쇄(印刷)(하)	printing
C	v 인식하다(認識-)[-시카-]	recognize
C	n 인연(因緣)[이년]	❶cause and occasion ❷ties
B	n 인원(人員)[이눤]	number of persons
C	n 인재(人材)	man of ability
C	v 인정되다(認定-)	be recognized
C	v 인정받다(認定-)[-따]	be acknowledged
C	v 인정하다(認定-)	acknowledge
C	n 인제	now
B	d 인제	❶right away ❷from now
C	n 인종(人種)	human race
A	n 인천(仁川)	Incheon
B	n 인천공항(仁川空港)	Incheon airport
C	n 인체(人體)	human body
B	n 인터넷(internet)	internet
B	n 인터뷰(interview)(하)	interview
C	n 인하(引下)(하)	reduction
C	v 인하다(因-)	be caused by
B	n 인형(人形)	❶doll ❷cat's paw

Korean Essential Vocabulary 6000 ✤ 301

A	n 일(하)	work
A	u 일(一)	one
A	n 일(日)	day
A	u 일곱	seven
B	n 일기(日氣)	weather
B	n 일기(日記)	diary
C	d 일단(一旦)[-딴]	❶ once
		❷ for the moment
C	r 일대(一大)[-때]	great
B	n 일등(一等)[-뜽]	first place
B	n 일반(一般)	whole
C	n 일반인(一般人)[-바닌]	public
B	n 일반적(一般的)	general
A	n 일본(日本)	Japan
A	n 일본어(日本語)[-보너]	Japanese language
B	n 일부(一部)	part
C	d 일부러	❶ especially
		❷ on purpose
B	n 일상(日常)[-쌍]	every day
B	n 일상생활(日常生活)[-쌍-]	daily life
C	n 일상적(日常的)[-쌍-]	daily

C	n	일생(一生)[-쌩]	one's (whole) life
C	n	일손[-쏜]	❶(work in) hand ❷skill ❸worker
C	n	일시적(一時的)[-씨-]	temporary
C	n	일식(日食)[-씩]	Japanese food
C	n	일쑤	habitual practice
A	v	일어나다[이러-]	❶stand up ❷get up
A	v	일어서다[이러-]	❶stand up ❷flourish
A	n	일요일(日曜日)[이료-]	Sunday
A	n	일월(一月)[이뤌]	January
B	v	일으키다[이르-]	set up
C	d	일일이[-리리]	one by one
C	n	일자(日子)[-짜]	date
C	n	일자리[-짜-]	job
B	n	일정(日程)[-쩡]	schedule
C	a	일정하다(一定-)[-쩡-]	(be) fixed
C	n	일종(一種)[-쫑]	kind
A	n	일주일(一週日)[-쭈-]	week
A	d	일찍	❶early ❷ever

C	d 일찍이[-찌기]	❶ early ❷ ever
C	n 일체(一切)	everything
C	n 일치(一致)(하)	agreement
C	v 일치하다(一致-)	accord
A	v 일하다	work
C	n 일행(一行)	party \<companion\>
B	n 일회용(一回用)	disposable
B	n 일회용품(一回用品)	disposable product
A	u 일흔	seventy
A	v 읽다[익따]	read
B	v 읽히다[일키-]	be read
A	v 잃다[일타]	❶ lose things ❷ lose (person) ❸ get lost
A	v 잃어버리다[이러-]	lose
C	n 임금	king
B	n 임금(賃金)	wage
C	n 임무(任務)	task
B	n 임시(臨時)	temporary
B	n 임신(妊娠)(하)	pregnancy

C n	임신부(妊娠婦)	pregnant woman
C v	임신하다(妊娠-)	be pregnant
A n	입	mouth
B n	입구(入口)[-꾸]	entrance
C n	입국(入國)(하)[-꾹]	entrance into a country
A v	입다[-따]	wear (clothes)
C n	입대(入隊)(하)[-때]	enrollment <army>
C n	입력(入力)(하)[임녁]	input
C v	입력하다(入力-)[임녀카-]	input
C n	입맛[임맏]	appetite
C n	입사(入社)(하)[-싸]	entering a company
C v	입사하다(入社-)[-싸-]	enter a company
B n	입술[-쑬]	lips
C n	입시(入試)[-씨]	entrance examination
B n	입원(入院)(하)[이붠]	hospitalization
B v	입원하다(入院-)[이붠-]	be hospitalized
C n	입장(立場)[-짱]	situation
B n	입학(入學)(하)[이팍]	admission to a

		school
B	v 입학하다(入學-)[이파카-]	enter a school
C	v 입히다[이피-]	make someone dressed
C	v 잇다[읻따]	❶ connect ❷ inherit
C	v 잇따르다[읻따-]	follow one after another
A	v 있다[읻따]	exist
A	s 있다[읻따]	…ing
A	v 잊다[읻따]	forget
A	v 잊어버리다[이저-]	forget
C	v 잊혀지다[이처-]	escape one's memory
A	n 잎[입]	leaf

ㅈ

C	ⓝ 자	Korean unit of length(30.3cm)
B	ⓔ 자	come on
C	ⓝ 자(字)	letter
C	ⓝ 자(者)	❶ person ❷ guy
B	ⓝ 자가용(自家用)	(for) private use
B	ⓝ 자격(資格)	qualification
C	ⓝ 자격증(資格證)[-쯩]	certificate of qualification
C	ⓝ 자극(刺戟)(하)	stimulus
C	ⓥ 자극하다(刺戟-)[-그카-]	stimulate
B	ⓝⓞ 자기(自己)	oneself
B	ⓓ 자꾸	frequently
B	ⓓ 자꾸만	frequently
C	ⓞ 자네	you
C	ⓝ 자녀(子女)	sons and daughters
A	ⓥ 자다	sleep
B	ⓝ 자동(自動)	automatic action

A	ⓝ 자동차(自動車)	automobile
B	ⓥ 자라나다	grow up
B	ⓥ 자라다	grow
C	ⓝ 자랑(하)	❶ pride ❷ brag
B	ⓐ 자랑스럽다[-따]	(be) proud of
B	ⓥ 자랑하다	take pride in
B	ⓝ 자료(資料)	data
B	ⓥ 자르다	cut
A	ⓝ 자리	bedding
C	ⓝ 자리	seat
C	ⓝ 자매(姉妹)	sisters
C	ⓝ 자부심(自負心)	self-conceit
C	ⓝ 자살(自殺)(하)	suicide
C	ⓥ 자살하다(自殺-)	kill oneself
C	ⓝ 자세(姿勢)	pose
C	ⓐ 자세하다(仔細-)	(be) detailed
B	ⓓ 자세히(仔細-)	minutely
B	ⓝ 자식(子息)	❶ offspring ❷ baby ❸ guy
B	ⓝ 자신(自身)	oneself
B	ⓝ 자신(自信)(하)	self-confidence

C	n 자신감(自信感)	confidence
B	n 자연(自然)	❶ nature
		❷ natural world
B	a 자연스럽다(自然-)[-따]	(be) natural
C	n 자연적(自然的)	natural
C	n 자연현상(自然現象)	natural phenomena
C	n 자연환경(自然環境)	natural environment
C	d 자연히(自然-)	naturally
C	n 자원(資源)	resources
B	n 자유(自由)	freedom
B	a 자유롭다(自由-)[-따]	(be) free
C	n 자율(自律)	self-control
A	n 자장면	noodles with stir-fried bean paste
A	n 자전거(自轉車)	bicycle
C	n 자정(子正)	midnight
C	n 자존심(自尊心)	self-respect
A	d 자주	often
B	n 자체(自體)	oneself

C	n 자취	trace
C	n 자판(字板)	keyboard
B	n 자판기(自販機)	vending machine
B	n 작가(作家)[-까]	author
A	n 작년(昨年)[장-]	last year
A	a 작다[-따]	(be) small
C	n 작성(作成)(하)[-썽]	drawing up
C	v 작성하다(作成-)[-썽-]	write out
B	v 작아지다[자가-]	become smaller
C	n 작업(作業)(하)[자겁]	work
C	n 작용(作用)(하)[자굥]	function
C	v 작용하다(作用-)[자굥-]	act
C	n 작은딸[자근-]	one's second daughter
C	n 작은아들[자근-]	one's second son
C	n 작은아버지[자근-]	younger brother of one's father
C	n 작은어머니[자근-]	wife of one's father's younger brother
C	n 작품(作品)	(piece of) work

A	n 잔(盞)	teacup
C	n 잔디	(a patch of) lawn
C	n 잔디밭[-받]	lawn
B	d 잔뜩	❶filled ❷full
B	n 잔치	feast
A	d 잘	❶nicely ❷exceedingly ❸exactly
C	a 잘나다[-라-]	❶(be) good-looking ❷(be) excellent
B	v 잘되다	go well
C	v 잘리다	❶be snapped ❷get fired
B	n 잘못[-몯]	fault
B	d 잘못[-몯]	by mistake
B	v 잘못되다[-몯뙤-]	go wrong
B	v 잘못하다[-모타-]	mistake
B	v 잘살다	live in plenty
B	a 잘생기다[-쌩-]	(be) handsome
A	v 잘하다	❶do well

A	n 잠	sleep
C	v 잠그다	lock
C	v 잠기다	sink
A	d 잠깐	for a moment
A	n 잠깐(暫間)	moment
B	v 잠들다	❶ fall asleep ❷ die
C	n 잠바(jumper)	jumper<clothes>
C	n 잠수함(潛水艦)	submarine
B	n d 잠시(暫時)	a short while, for a while
B	n 잠옷[자몯]	pajamas
A	v 잠자다	sleep
C	n 잠자리	dragonfly
C	n 잠자리[-짜-]	sleeping place
A	v 잡다[-따]	❶ catch ❷ fix ❸ assume ❷ be skillful
C	v 잡수다[-쑤-]	honorific of eat
A	v 잡수시다[-쑤-]	honorific of eat
C	v 잡아당기다[자바-]	pull

C ⓥ	잡아먹다[자바-]	❶butcher and eat ❷waste
A ⓝ	잡지(雜誌)[-찌]	magazine
B ⓥ	잡히다[자피-]	be caught
B ⓝ	장	chapter
A ⓝ	장(張)	sheet (of paper)
B ⓝ	장가	getting a bride
B ⓝ	장갑(掌甲)	gloves
C ⓝ	장관(長官)	❶minister ❷ancient government position
B ⓝ	장군(將軍)	general(soldier)
C ⓝ	장기간(長期間)	for long
C ⓝ	장기적(長期的)	long-range
C ⓝ	장난(하)	❶toy ❷joke ❸mischief
B ⓝ	장난감[-깜]	toy
B ⓝ	장남(長男)	eldest son
B ⓝ	장래(將來)[-내]	future
C ⓝ	장례(葬禮)(하)[-네]	funeral
C ⓝ	장례식(葬禮式)[-네-]	funeral services

C	ⓝ 장르(프genre)	genre
B	ⓝ 장마	rainy spell in summer
C	ⓝ 장면(場面)	scene
C	ⓝ 장모(丈母)	wife's mother
C	ⓝ 장모님(丈母-)	honorific word of wife's mother
A	ⓝ 장미(薔薇)	rose
C	ⓝ 장비(裝備)	equipment
B	ⓝ 장사(하)	business
C	ⓝ 장사꾼	vulgar word of merchant
A	ⓝ 장소(場所)	place
C	ⓝ 장수	tradesman
C	ⓝ 장식(裝飾)(하)	decorating
C	ⓝ 장애(障碍)	hindrance, troubles
C	ⓝ 장인(丈人)	craftsman
B	ⓝ 장점(長點)[-쩜]	strong point
C	ⓓ 장차(將次)	in the future
B	ⓝ 장학금(獎學金)[-끔]	scholarship
C	ⓐ 잦다[잗따]	(be) frequent

C	ⓝ 재능(才能)	talent
C	ⓥ 재다	❶ measure ❷ weigh
B	ⓝ 재료	material
A	ⓝ 재미	amusement
A	ⓐ 재미없다[-업따]	(be) uninteresting
A	ⓐ 재미있다[-잇따]	(be) interesting
C	ⓐ 재밌다[-믿따]	(be) interesting
C	ⓓ 재빨리	quickly
B	ⓝ 재산(財産)	property
C	ⓝ 재생(再生)(하)	❶ restoration to life ❷ playback
C	ⓝ 재수(財數)	fortune
C	ⓥ 재우다	mix up meat with seasoning
B	ⓝ 재작년(再昨年)[-장-]	year before last
C	ⓝ 재정(財政)	finances
C	ⓝ 재주	ability
C	ⓝ 재즈(jazz)	jazz
B	ⓝ 재채기	sneeze
C	ⓝ 재판(裁判)(하)	❶ judgement

		❷justice
C	ⓝ재학(在學)(하)	being in school
C	ⓝ재활용(再活用)(하)[-화룡]	recycling
C	ⓝ재활용품(再活用品)[-화룡-]	recyclable material
A	ⓞ저	that
A	ⓞ저	I (familiar word)
A	ⓡ저	that
B	ⓔ저	well
A	ⓞ저거	that
A	ⓞ저것[-걷]	that
C	ⓝ저고리	Korean jacket
A	ⓞ저곳[-곧]	there
C	ⓔ저기	I say
A	ⓞ저기	there
A	ⓝ저녁	evening
B	ⓝ저녁때	evening (time)
C	ⓥ저러다	do like that
B	ⓔ저런	Oh dear
B	ⓡ저런	that (kind of)
B	ⓓ저렇게[-러케]	like that

B ⓐ	저렇다[-러타]	(be) like that
B ⓓ	저리	like that
C ⓓ	저마다	each one
B ⓝ	저번(這番)	last time
C ⓝ	저울	scales
B ⓝ	저자(著者)	writer
C ⓓ	저절로	of itself
C ⓥ	저지르다	commit (an error)
A ⓞ	저쪽	that side
B ⓝ	저축(貯蓄)(하)	savings
C ⓞ	저편(-便)	that side
B ⓞ	저희	we(familiar term)
B ⓝ	적	the time when
B ⓝ	적(敵)	enemy
B ⓝ	적극(積極)[-끅]	positiveness
B ⓝ	적극적(積極的)[-끅쩍]	positive
A ⓥ	적다[-따]	write
A ⓐ	적다[-따]	(be) little
B ⓐ	적당하다(適當-)[-땅-]	(be) suitable
B ⓓ	적당히(適當-)[-땅-]	suitably
C ⓝ	적성(適性)[-썽]	aptitude

B	d	적어도[저거-]	at least
B	v	적어지다[저거-]	decrease
C	n	적용(適用)(하)[저꽁]	❶ application ❷ admission
C	v	적용되다(適用-)[저꽁-]	be applied
B	v	적용하다(適用-)[저꽁-]	apply
C	n	적응(適應)(하)[저긍]	adaptation
C	v	적응하다(適應-)[저긍-]	be adapted to
C	a	적절하다(適切-)[-쩔-]	(be) proper
C	a	적합하다(適合-)[저카파-]	(be) fit
C	v	적히다[저키-]	be recorded
C	r	전(全)	entire
A	n	전(前)	before
A	r	전(前)	former
C	n	전개(展開)(하)	development
C	v	전개되다(展開-)	be developed
C	v	전개하다(展開-)	develop
B	n	전공(專攻)(하)	major
C	v	전공하다(專攻-)	major
C	n	전구(電球)	electric bulb
B	n	전국(全國)	whole country

C ⓝ	전국적(全國的)[-쩍]	national
C ⓝ	전기(傳記)	electricity
C ⓝ	전기(前期)	former term
B ⓝ	전기(電氣)	electricity
B ⓝ	전기밥솥(電氣)[-쏟]	electric rice-cooker
B ⓝ	전날(前-)	other day
C ⓝ	전달(傳達)(하)	delivery
C ⓥ	전달되다(傳達-)	be delivered
B ⓥ	전달하다(傳達-)	deliver
B ⓝ	전라도(全羅道)[절-]	Jeolla-do <administrative district>
C ⓝ	전망(展望)(하)	❶ view ❷ forecast
C ⓥ	전망하다(展望-)	forecast
B ⓝ	전문(專門)(하)	specialty
B ⓝ	전문가(專門家)	specialist
C ⓝ	전문적(專門的)	special
C ⓝ	전문점(專門店)	specialty store
C ⓝ	전문직(專門職)	professional
C ⓝ	전반(全般)	whole
C ⓝ	전반적(全般的)	overall

B ⓝ	전부(全部)	entire
B ⓓ	전부(全部)	entirely
C ⓝ	전선(戰線)	battle line
C ⓝ	전설(傳說)	legend
C ⓝ	전세(傳貰)	lease of a house on a deposit basis
C ⓝ	전시(展示)(하)	exhibition
C ⓥ	전시되다	be displayed
C ⓝ	전시장(展示場)	exhibition hall
C ⓥ	전시하다(展示-)	display
C ⓝ	전시회(展示會)	exhibition
C ⓝ	전용(專用)(하)[저농]	exclusive use
B ⓝ	전자(電子)	electron
B ⓝ	전쟁(戰爭)(하)	war
C ⓝ	전주(全州)	Jeonju
B ⓝ	전철(電鐵)	electric railway
B ⓝ	전체(全體)	totality
B ⓝ	전체적(全體的)	total
B ⓝ	전통(傳統)	tradition
C ⓝ	전통문화(傳統文化)	traditional culture
B ⓝ	전통적(傳統的)	traditional

B Ⓥ	전하다(傳-)	❶ deliver
		❷ hand down
B Ⓥ	전해지다(傳-)	come down
B Ⓓ	전혀(全-)	completely
A Ⓝ	전화(電話)(하)	phone
B Ⓝ	전화기(電話機)	telephone
A Ⓝ	전화번호(電話番號)	telephone number
A Ⓥ	전화하다(電話-)	telephone
C Ⓝ	전환(轉換)(하)	conversion
C Ⓥ	전환하다(轉換-)	convert
C Ⓝ	전후(前後)	❶ front and rear
		❷ right and left
B Ⓝ	절(하)	salute
B Ⓝ	절	Buddhist temple
C Ⓝ	절(節)	clause
B Ⓓ	절대(絕對)[-때]	absolutely
C Ⓝ	절대(絕對)[-때]	absoluteness
B Ⓓ	절대로(絕對-)[-때-]	absolutely
C Ⓝ	절대적(絕對的)[-때-]	absolute
C Ⓝ	절망(絕望)(하)	hopelessness
B Ⓝ	절반(折半)(하)	half

C	ⓝ 절약(節約)(하)[-략]	thrift
B	ⓥ 절약하다(節約-)[저랴카-]	save
C	ⓝ 절차(節次)	procedure
B	ⓐ 젊다[점따]	(be) young
B	ⓝ 젊은이[절므니]	young person
C	ⓝ 젊음[절믐]	youth
B	ⓝ 점(點)	dot
B	ⓝ 점(點)	❶ point ❷ piece
C	ⓝ 점검(點檢)(하)	check
B	ⓝ 점수(點數)[-쑤]	grade
A	ⓝ 점심(點心)	lunch
B	ⓝ 점심때(點心-)	lunchtime
A	ⓝ 점심시간(點心時間)	noon recess
B	ⓝ 점원(店員)[저뭔]	clerk
C	ⓐ 점잖다[-잔타]	(be) dignified
B	ⓓ 점점(漸漸)	more and more
B	ⓓ 점차(漸次)	gradually
C	ⓝ 접근(接近)(하)[-끈]	approach
C	ⓥ 접근하다(接近-)[-끈-]	approach
C	ⓥ 접다[-따]	❶ fold ❷ wrap
B	ⓝ 접시[-씨]	dish

C	ⓝ 접촉(接觸)(하)	contact
C	ⓥ 접하다(接-)[저파-]	❶ border ❷ touch, receive
A	ⓝ 젓가락[저까-]	chopsticks
B	ⓥ 젓다[젇따]	❶ wave ❷ beat
B	ⓝ 정(情)	❶ one's heart ❷ emotion
B	ⓝ 정거장(停車場)	railroad station
C	ⓝ 정기(定期)	regular interval
C	ⓝ 정기적(定期的)	regular
B	ⓝ 정답(正答)	correct answer
C	ⓝ 정당(政黨)	political party
B	ⓝ 정도(程度)	degree
A	ⓝ 정류장(停留場)[-뉴-]	stop
B	ⓝ 정리(整理)(하)[-니]	arrangement
C	ⓥ 정리되다(整理-)[-니-]	be arranged
B	ⓥ 정리하다(整理-)[-니-]	arrange
B	ⓝ 정말(正-)	reality
B	ⓔ 정말(正-)	really
A	ⓓ 정말(正-)	really
B	ⓓ 정말로(正-)	really

C ⓝ 정면(正面)	front side
B ⓝ 정문(正門)	main gate
C ⓝ 정반대(正反對)	opposite
B ⓝ 정보(情報)	information
C ⓝ 정보화(情報化)	information-oriented
C ⓝ 정부(政府)	government
C ⓝ 정비(整備)(하)	❶maintenance ❷servicing
C ⓝ 정상(正常)	normality
B ⓝ 정상(頂上)	summit
C ⓝ 정상적(正常的)	normal
C ⓝ 정성(精誠)	true heart
B ⓝ 정식(正式)	formality
B ⓝ 정신(精神)	mind
C ⓝ 정신과(精神科)[-꽈]	department of psychiatry
C ⓓ 정신없이(精神-)[-시넙씨]	delirious
B ⓝ 정신적(精神的)	mental
C ⓝ 정오(正午)	noon
B ⓝ 정원(庭園)	garden

C	n 정장(正裝)	suit
C	n 정지(停止)(하)	stop
C	a 정직하다(正直-)[-지카-]	(be) honest
B	n 정치(政治)(하)	politics
C	n 정치권(政治權)[-꿘]	political circle
C	n 정치인(政治人)	politician
B	n 정치적(政治的)	political
C	n 정치학(政治學)	political science
B	v 정하다(定-)	❶ decide ❷ settle
B	v 정해지다(定-)	be decided
B	a 정확하다(正確-)[-화카-]	(be) correct
B	d 정확히(正確-)[-화키]	rightly
C	n 젖[젇]	breast
B	v 젖다[전따]	get wet
C	v 제거하다(除去-)	remove
C	n 제공(提供)(하)	offer
B	v 제공하다(提供-)	provide
C	n 제과점(製菓店)	bakery
B	d 제대로	❶ smoothly ❷ as it is
C	v 제대하다(除隊-)	be discharged

		from military service
C n	제도적(制度的)	institutional
B n	제목(題目)	title
B d	제발	please
B d	제법	quite
C n	제비	swallow
C n	제사(祭祀)(하)	religious service
C n	제삿날(祭祀-)[-산-]	sacrificial day
C n	제시(提示)(하)	presentation
C v	제시되다(提示-)	be presented
C v	제시하다(提示-)	present
C n	제안(提案)(하)	suggestion
C v	제안하다(提案-)	propose
C n	제약(制約)(하)	restriction
C v	제외되다(除外-)	be excluded
C v	제외하다(除外-)	exclude
C n	제의(提議)(하)[-이]	proposal
C v	제의하다(提議-)[-이-]	suggest
A n	제일(第一)	number one
C n	제자(弟子)	pupil

C	n 제자리	original place
C	n 제작(製作)(하)	manufacture
C	v 제작하다(製作-)[-자카-]	manufacture
A	n 제주도(濟州島)	Jeju-do
C	n 제출(提出)(하)	submission
B	v 제출하다(提出-)	submit
B	n 제품(製品)	product
B	n 제한(制限)(하)	limitation
C	v 제한되다(制限-)	be restricted
C	v 제한하다(制限-)	restrict
C	n 조(條)	article(of law)
C	n 조(組)	team
C	n 조(組)	team
C	n 조각	piece
B	n 조각(彫刻)(하)	carving
C	n 조개	clam
B	n 조건(條件)[-껀]	condition
C	a 조그마하다	(be) small
B	a 조그맣다[-마타]	(be) small
A	d 조금	❶ a little
		❷ somewhat

A ⓝ 조금	a little
B ⓓ 조금씩	little by little
C ⓝ 조기(早期)	early period
C ⓝ 조깅(jogging)(하)	jogging
C ⓥ 조르다	tease (for)
C ⓝ 조명(照明)	❶ lighting ❷ light
C ⓝ 조미료(調味料)	spices
B ⓝ 조사(調査)(하)	survey
B ⓥ 조사하다(調査-)	investigate
B ⓝ 조상(祖上)	ancestor
C ⓝ 조선(朝鮮)	Joseon
B ⓐ 조심스럽다(操心-)[-따]	(be) careful
B ⓥ 조심하다(操心-)	be careful
A ⓐ 조용하다(從容-)	❶ (be) quiet ❷ (be) smooth ❸ (be) calm
B ⓓ 조용히	❶ quietly ❷ peacefully
C ⓝ 조절(調節)(하)	control
C ⓥ 조절하다(調節-)	regulate
C ⓝ 조정(調整)(하)	adjustment

C	ⓥ 조정하다(調整-)	adjust
C	ⓝ 조직(組織)(하)	organization
B	ⓝ 조카	nephew
C	ⓥ 조화되다(調和-)	harmonize
C	ⓥ 존경하다(尊敬-)	respect
B	ⓝ 존댓말(尊待-)[-댄-]	honorific word
C	ⓝ 존재(存在)(하)	❶ existence ❷ person
C	ⓥ 존재하다(存在-)	exist
C	ⓥ 존중하다(尊重-)	esteem
B	ⓥ 졸다	doze
C	ⓥ 졸리다	feel sleepy
A	ⓝ 졸업(卒業)(하)[조럽]	graduation
B	ⓝ 졸업생(卒業生)[조럽쌩]	graduate
A	ⓥ 졸업하다(卒業-)[조러파-]	graduate
C	ⓝ 졸음[조름]	sleepiness
A	ⓓ 좀	a little
B	ⓐ 좁다[-따]	(be) narrow
C	ⓥ 좁히다[조피-]	restrict
B	ⓝ 종(種)	seed
C	ⓝ 종(鐘)	bell

B	ⓝ 종교(宗敎)	religion
C	ⓝ 종교적(宗敎的)	religious
B	ⓝ 종로(鍾路)[-노]	Jongno
B	ⓝ 종류(種類)[-뉴]	sort
C	ⓝ 종소리(鐘-)[-쏘-]	sound of a bell
B	ⓝ 종업원(從業員)[-어뿬]	employee
A	ⓝ 종이	paper
B	ⓝ 종이컵(-cup)	paper cup
B	ⓝ 종일(終日)	all day long
C	ⓓ 종종(種種)	occasionally
B	ⓝ 종합(綜合)(하)	synthesis
C	ⓥ 종합하다(綜合-)[-하파-]	synthesize
A	ⓐ 좋다[조타]	❶(be) good
		❷(be) happy
C	ⓔ 좋아[조-]	O.K.
B	ⓥ 좋아지다[조-]	get better
A	ⓥ 좋아하다[조-]	like
B	ⓝ 좌석(座席)	seat
C	ⓝ 좌우(左右)	right and left
C	ⓝ 죄(罪)	crime
A	ⓐ 죄송하다(罪悚-)	(be) sorry

C	n	죄인(罪人)	criminal
C	r	주(主)	main
A	n	주(週)	week
A	n	주(週)	week<counting>
C	n	주거(住居)(하)	habitation
C	v	주고받다[-따]	❶exchange ❷talk
C	n	주관적(主觀的)	subjective
C	n	주년(周年)	whole year
A	s	주다	provide for
A	v	주다	❶give ❷confer ❸water
B	d	주로(主-)	mainly
C	n	주름	creases
C	n	주름살[-쌀]	wrinkles
A	n	주말(週末)	weekend
B	n	주머니	pocket
B	n	주먹	fist
B	v	주무시다	honorific of go to bed
C	n	주문(呪文)	magic formula

C	ⓝ 주문(注文)(하)	ordering
B	ⓥ 주문하다(注文-)	order
C	ⓝ 주민(住民)	residents
C	ⓝ 주방(廚房)	kitchen
B	ⓝ 주변(周邊)	circumference
B	ⓝ 주부(主婦)	housewife
B	ⓝ 주사(注射)(하)	injection
A	ⓝ 주소(住所)	address
A	ⓝ 주스(juice)	juice
C	ⓝ 주식(株式)	stocks
C	ⓥ 주어지다	in being
B	ⓝ 주요(主要)	principal
C	ⓐ 주요하다(主要-)	(be) principal
B	ⓝ 주위(周圍)	circumference
C	ⓝ 주의(注意)(하)[-이]	❶attention ❷carefulness
C	ⓥ 주의하다(注意-)[-이-]	be careful of
A	ⓝ 주인(主人)	owner (of goods)
B	ⓝ 주인공(主人公)	hero, heroine
C	ⓝ 주일(週日)	week
C	ⓝ 주장(主張)(하)	assertion

B	ⓥ 주장하다(主張-)	assert
C	ⓥ 주저앉다[-안따]	❶ plump down ❷ stay on
C	ⓝ 주전자(酒煎子)	kettle
B	ⓝ 주제(主題)	theme
B	ⓝ 주차(駐車)(하)	parking
B	ⓝ 주차장(駐車場)	parking place
B	ⓥ 주차하다(駐車-)	park
B	ⓝ 주택(住宅)	(dwelling) house
C	ⓝ 주한(駐韓)	stationed in Korea
C	ⓓ 죽	❶ throughout ❷ with drip
B	ⓝ 죽(粥)	(rice) gruel
B	ⓢ 죽다[-따]	be dying to
A	ⓥ 죽다[-따]	die
B	ⓝ 죽음[주금]	death
B	ⓥ 죽이다[주기-]	kill
A	ⓝ 준비(準備)(하)	preparation
B	ⓥ 준비되다(準備-)	be prepared
B	ⓝ 준비물(準備物)	spare

A	ⓥ 준비하다(準備-)	prepare
B	ⓝ 줄	rope
B	ⓝ 줄	row
C	ⓝ 줄거리	❶ stem ❷ trunk ❸ plot
C	ⓓ 줄곧	all the time
B	ⓝ 줄기	❶ trunk ❷ range(mountain), course(river)
B	ⓥ 줄다	❶ reduce ❷ degenerate
B	ⓝ 줄무늬[-니]	stripe
C	ⓥ 줄어들다[주러-]	decrease
B	ⓥ 줄이다[주리-]	reduce
B	ⓥ 줍다[-따]	pick up
B	ⓝ 중(中)	among
B	ⓝ 중간(中間)	middle
C	ⓝ 중계방송(中繼放送)[-게-]	hook-up
A	ⓝ 중국(中國)	China
A	ⓝ 중국어(中國語)[-구거]	Chinese language
B	ⓝ 중국집(中國-)[-찝]	Chinese place

C	n 중년(中年)	middle age
C	n 중단(中斷)(하)	discontinuance
C	v 중단되다(中斷-)	be discontinued
C	v 중단하다(中斷-)	discontinue
C	a 중대하다(重大-)	(be) momentous
C	n 중독(中毒)	poisoning
C	n 중반(中盤)	middle (of an era)
C	n 중부(中部)	central part
C	n 중세(中世)	Middle Ages
C	n 중소기업(中小企業)	small and medium enterprises
C	n 중순(中旬)	second ten days of a month
C	n 중식(中食)	Chinese dishes
B	n 중심(中心)	center
C	n 중심지(中心地)	central place
C	n 중앙(中央)	❶ center ❷ middle
C	v 중얼거리다	murmur
B	n 중요(重要)(하)	importance
B	n 중요성(重要性)[-썽]	importance

C	v 중요시하다(重要視-)	attach great importance to
A	a 중요하다(重要-)	(be) important
A	n 중학교(中學校)[-꾜]	middle school
A	n 중학생(中學生)[-쌩]	middle school student
B	n 쥐	mouse
B	v 쥐다	❶hold ❷grasp
B	d 즉(即)	in other words
C	n 즉석(即席)[-썩]	instant
B	n 즉시(即時)[-씨]	instantly
B	n 즐거움	pleasure
B	v 즐거워하다	be delighted
A	a 즐겁다[-따]	(be) pleasant
B	v 즐기다	❶enjoy ❷be happy
C	n 증가(增加)(하)	increase
C	v 증가하다(增加-)	increase
C	n 증거(證據)	evidence
C	n 증권(證券)[-꿘]	certificate of stock share

C n	증권사(證券社)[-꿘-]	stock company
C v	증명하다(證明-)	prove
B n	증상(症狀)	symptoms
B n	증세(症勢)	symptoms
B n	지	since, after
C n	지각(知覺)(하)	perception
A n	지갑(紙匣)	purse
C a	지겹다[-따]	(be) tedious
C n	지경(地境)	❶ border
		❷ situation
B n	지구(地區)	zone
B n	지구(地球)	earth
C d	지극히(至極-)[-그키]	exceedingly
A n	지금(只今)	present (time)
A d	지금(只今)	(just) in a moment
C d	지금껏(只今-)[-껃]	so far
C n	지급(支給)(하)	supply
C v	지급하다(支給-)[-그파-]	supply
B v	지나가다	pass by
B v	지나다	pass by
C v	지나치다	go too far

B ⓐ	지나치다	(be) excessive
C ⓝ	지난날	old days
A ⓝ	지난달	last month
B ⓝ	지난번(-番)	last time
A ⓝ	지난주(-週)	last week
B ⓝ	지난해	last year
A ⓥ	지내다	spend (one's time)
C ⓝ	지능(知能)	intelligence
C ⓥ	지니다	❶carry ❷endow
B ⓥ	지다	be gone
B ⓥ	지다	face away
C ⓥ	지다	be defeated
B ⓥ	지다	lose
C ⓝ	지대(地帶)	zone
A ⓝ	지도(地圖)	map
C ⓝ	지도(指導)(하)	guidance
C ⓝ	지도자(指導者)	leader
C ⓥ	지도하다(指導-)	guide
C ⓐ	지루하다	❶(be) boring ❷(be) insipid

B Ⓥ	지르다	yell
C Ⓝ	지름길[-낄]	shortcut
C Ⓝ	지리산(智異山)	Mt.Jiri
B Ⓝ	지방(地方)	❶ district
		❷ country
C Ⓝ	지방(脂肪)	fat
C Ⓥ	지배하다(支配-)	❶ dominate
		❷ direct
C Ⓥ	지불하다(支拂-)	pay
B Ⓝ	지붕	roof
C Ⓥ	지속되다(持續-)	continue
C Ⓝ	지속적(持續的)[-쩍]	continual
C Ⓝ	지시(指示)(하)	directions
C Ⓥ	지시하다(指示-)	direct
C Ⓝ	지식(知識)	knowledge
C Ⓝ	지식인(知識人)[-시긴]	intellectual (person)
B Ⓝ	지역(地域)	area
A Ⓝ	지우개	eraser
A Ⓥ	지우다	erase
C Ⓥ	지워지다	wipe out

C	n 지원(支援)(하)	support
C	v 지원하다(支援-)	apply for
C	n 지위(地位)	status
C	a 지저분하다	❶(be) disordered ❷(be) dirty
C	n 지적(指摘)(하)	indication
C	n 지적(知的)[-쩍]	intellectual
C	v 지적되다(指摘-)	be pointed out
C	v 지적하다(指摘-)[-저카-]	point out
B	n 지점(地點)	point
C	n 지점(支店)	branch office
C	n 지지(支持)(하)	support
C	n 지진(地震)	earthquake
C	n 지출(支出)(하)	expenses
B	v 지치다	❶exhaust oneself ❷be dreary
C	v 지켜보다	stare
B	v 지키다	❶defend ❷keep
C	n 지폐(紙幣)[-폐]	paper money
A	n 지하(地下)	underground
B	n 지하도(地下道)	underground

		passage
A	n 지하철(地下鐵)	subway
C	n 지혜(智慧)[-헤]	wisdom
C	n 직선(直線)[-썬]	straight line
B	n 직업(職業)[지겁]	job
B	n 직원(職員)[지권]	employee
B	n 직장(職場)[-짱]	one's work place
C	n 직장인(職場人)[-짱-]	office worker
C	n 직전(直前)[-쩐]	just before
B	n 직접(直接)[-쩝]	directly
B	d 직접(直接)[-쩝]	immediateness
C	n 직접적(直接的)[-쩝쩍]	direct
C	n 직후(直後)[지후]	immediately
C	n 진급(進級)(하)	promotion
C	n 진단(診斷)(하)	diagnosis
C	v 진단하다(診斷-)	diagnose
B	n 진달래	azalea <flower>
C	n 진동(振動)(하)	vibration
C	n 진로(進路)[질-]	course
C	n 진료(診療)(하)[질-]	medical examination and treatment

C	ⓝ 진리(眞理)[질-]	truth
C	ⓝ 진실(眞實)(하)	fact
C	ⓓ 진실로(眞實-)	sincerely
C	ⓐ 진실하다(眞實-)	(be) truthful
C	ⓝ 진심(眞心)	true heart
C	ⓐ 진지하다(眞摯-)	(be) sincere
B	ⓝ 진짜(眞-)	real thing
B	ⓓ 진짜(眞-)	genuinely
C	ⓝ 진찰(診察)(하)	medical examination
B	ⓝ 진출(進出)(하)	advance
C	ⓥ 진출하다(進出-)	advance
C	ⓝ 진통(陣痛)(하)	labor pains
B	ⓐ 진하다(津-)	❶(be) dark <color> ❷(be) thick <gravy>
C	ⓝ 진행(進行)(하)	progress
B	ⓥ 진행되다(進行-)	progress
C	ⓝ 진행자(進行者)	MC
B	ⓥ 진행하다(進行-)	progress

B	n 질(質)	① quality ② temperament
A	n 질문(質問)(하)	question
A	v 질문하다(質問-)	ask
C	n 질병(疾病)	disease
B	n 질서(秩序)[-써]	(public) order
C	n 질적(質的)[-쩍]	qualitative
B	n 짐	① baggage ② responsibility, charge
C	n 짐작(斟酌)(하)	guess
C	v 짐작하다(斟酌-)[-자카-]	guess
A	n 집	① house ② nest
B	v 집다[-따]	① raise something with utensil ② pick up
C	n 집단(集團)[-딴]	group
C	n 집단적(集團的)[-딴-]	collective
B	n 집안[지반]	① indoors ② relatives
C	n 집안일[지반닐]	housework

C	ⓥ 집어넣다[지버너타]	throw into
B	ⓝ 집중(集中)(하)[-쭝]	concentration
C	ⓥ 집중되다(集中-)[-쭝-]	concentrate
C	ⓝ 집중적(集中的)[-쭝-]	concentrative
C	ⓥ 집중하다(集中-)[-쭝-]	concentrate
B	ⓝ 짓[짇]	act
B	ⓥ 짓다[짇따]	❶ manufacture
		❷ build
B	ⓐ 짙다[짇따]	❶ (be) dark
		❷ (be) thick
C	ⓥ 짚다[집따]	❶ use ❷ put
		❸ feel
C	ⓥ 짜다	compress
A	ⓐ 짜다	(be) salty
C	ⓥ 짜다	❶ construct
		❷ form
B	ⓝ 짜증	irritability
C	ⓐ 짜증스럽다[-따]	(be) annoyed
C	ⓝ 짝	one of a pair
A	ⓐ 짧다[짤따]	(be) short
B	ⓥ 짧아지다[짤바-]	shorten

C Ⓥ 쩔쩔매다	❶ be pressed with
	❷ be confused
C Ⓝ 쪽	edge
B Ⓝ 쪽	page
A Ⓝ 쪽	slice
C Ⓥ 쫓겨나다[쫃껴–]	be ejected
C Ⓥ 쫓기다[쫃끼–]	be chased
C Ⓥ 쫓다[쫃따]	❶ drive away
	❷ chase
C Ⓓ 쭉	❶ with a drip
	❷ in a row
A Ⓝ 찌개	pot stew
C Ⓝ 찌꺼기	❶ dreg
	❷ worthless
B Ⓥ 찌다	gain weight
C Ⓥ 찌다	steam
B Ⓥ 찌르다	❶ thrust ❷ prick
A Ⓥ 찍다	stamp
C Ⓥ 찍히다[찌키–]	be sealed
C Ⓥ 찢다[찓따]	be torn
C Ⓥ 찢어지다[찌저–]	be torn

ㅊ

C	n 차	time
C	n 차(差)	difference
A	n 차(茶)	tea
A	n 차(車)	vehicle
B	a 차갑다[-따]	❶(be) cold
		❷(be) cold-hearted
B	n 차남(次男)	one's second son
B	v 차다	be full of
B	a 차다	(be) cold
C	v 차다	kick
C	v 차다	wear (bracelet)
C	d 차라리	rather (than)
C	n 차량(車輛)	vehicles
B	n 차례(次例)	❶order
		❷time, round
B	v 차리다	❶set ❷establish
C	n 차림	dress
C	d 차마	for (all) the world

C	ⓝ 차별(差別)(하)	discrimination
C	ⓝ 차선(車線)	(traffic) line
B	ⓝ 차이(差異)	difference
C	ⓝ 차이점(差異點)[-쩜]	point of difference
C	ⓓ 차차(次次)	❶ gradually ❷ slowly
C	ⓝ 차창(車窓)	car window
C	ⓓ 차츰	gradually
C	ⓝ 착각(錯覺)[-깍]	illusion
C	ⓥ 착각하다(錯覺-)[-까카-]	misunderstand
B	ⓐ 착하다[차카-]	(be) good
B	ⓝ 찬물	cold water
C	ⓝ 찬성(贊成)(하)	approval
C	ⓥ 찬성하다(贊成-)	approve
A	ⓓ 참	really
B	ⓔ 참	ugh
C	ⓝ 참	❶ moment ❷ plan
C	ⓝ 참가(參加)(하)	participation
B	ⓥ 참가하다(參加-)	join
C	ⓥ 참고하다(參考-)	refer to
B	ⓝ 참기름	sesame oil

B	ⓥ 참다[-따]	endure
C	ⓐ 참되다	(be) true
C	ⓝ 참새	sparrow
C	ⓝ 참석(參席)(하)	attendance
C	ⓝ 참석자(參席者)[-짜]	attendant
B	ⓥ 참석하다(參席-)[-서카-]	attend
C	ⓝ 참여(參與)(하)[차며]	participation
C	ⓥ 참여하다(參與-)[차며-]	participate
C	ⓝ 참외[차뫼]	melon
C	ⓓ 참으로[차므-]	truly
C	ⓝ 참조(參照)(하)	reference
B	ⓝ 찻잔(茶盞)[차짠]	teacup
C	ⓝ 창(窓)	window
C	ⓝ 창가(窓-)[-까]	by the window
B	ⓝ 창고(倉庫)[-꼬]	warehouse
C	ⓝ 창구(窓口)[-꾸]	wicket
A	ⓝ 창문(窓門)	window
B	ⓝ 창밖(窓-)[-박]	outside the window
C	ⓝ 창작(創作)(하)	origination
C	ⓝ 창조(創造)(하)	creation

C n	창조적(創造的)	creational
C v	창조하다(創造-)	create
C a	창피하다(猖披-)	(be) ashamed
A v	찾다[찬따]	❶search ❷draw
B v	찾아가다[차자-]	go and see
B v	찾아내다[차자-]	find out
C v	찾아다니다[차자-]	search
B v	찾아보다[차자-]	try to look for
B v	찾아오다[차자-]	come to see
C n	채	counting unit of house
C n	채	keep original condition
C d	채	still
B n	채널(channel)	channel
B n	채소(菜蔬)	vegetable
B v	채우다	❶lock ❷fasten (button)
C n	채점(採點)(하)[-쩜]	scoring
A n	책(冊)	❶book ❷volume
B n	책가방(冊-)[-까-]	satchel

B n	책방(册房)[-빵]	bookstore
A n	책상(册床)[-쌍]	desk
B n	책임(責任)[채김]	responsibility
C n	책임감(責任感)[채김-]	sense of responsibility
B n	책임자(責任者)[채김-]	responsible person
C v	책임지다[채김-]	assume the responsibility
B n	챔피언(champion)	champion
B v	챙기다	❶ put in order ❷ settle
C n	처녀(處女)	❶ virgin ❷ first
C n	처리(處理)(하)	handling
C n	처벌(處罰)(하)	punishment
A n	처음(初次)	beginning
C n	처지(處地)	situation
C n	척	pretense
C n	척(隻)	ships
C s	척하다[처카-]	pretend
C n	천	cloth

A Ⓤ 천(千)	thousand
A Ⓡ 천(千)	thousand
C Ⓝ 천국(天國)	heaven
C Ⓝ 천둥	thunder
C Ⓝ 천장(天障)	ceiling
C Ⓝ 천재(天才)	genius
A Ⓓ 천천히	slowly
B Ⓝ 철	season
C Ⓝ 철	discretion
C Ⓝ 철(鐵)	iron
C Ⓝ 철도(鐵道)[-또]	railroad
C Ⓐ 철저하다(徹底-)[-쩌-]	(be) thorough
C Ⓓ 철저히(徹底-)[-쩌-]	thoroughly
C Ⓝ 철학(哲學)	philosophy
C Ⓝ 철학자(哲學者)[-짜]	philosopher
C Ⓝ 철학적(哲學的)[-쩍]	philosophical
B Ⓡ 첫[천]	first
B Ⓝ 첫날[천-]	first day
A Ⓡ 첫째[천-]	first
B Ⓝ 청년(靑年)	young man
A Ⓝ 청바지(靑-)	blue jeans

A	n 청소(淸掃)(하)	cleaning
B	n 청소기(淸掃機)	cleaner
B	n 청소년(靑少年)	teenagers
A	v 청소하다(淸掃-)	clean
C	n 청춘(靑春)	youth
C	v 청하다(請-)	❶ require ❷ invite
C	n 체계적(體系的)[-게-]	systematical
C	n 체력(體力)	physical strength
C	n 체온(體溫)	(body) temperature
B	n 체육(體育)	physical exercise
C	n 체육관(體育館)[-꽌]	gymnasium
C	n 체조(體操)(하)	gymnastics
B	n 체중(體重)	(body) weight
C	s 체하다	pretend
C	n 체험(體驗)(하)	(one's personal) experience
C	v 체험하다(體驗-)	undergo
B	v 쳐다보다[처-]	look up
B	n 초(初)	beginning
B	n 초(秒)	second <time>

C	n 초기(初期)	early days
C	n 초대(初代)	first generation
A	n 초대(招待)(하)	invitation
A	v 초대하다(招待-)	invite
A	n 초등학교(初等學校)[-꾜]	elementary school
C	n 초등학생(初等學生)[-쌩]	elementary school student
B	n 초록색(草綠色)[-쌕]	green color
C	n 초반(初盤)	opening part (of a game)
B	n 초밥(醋-)	sushi
B	n 초보(初步)	first steps
B	n 초보자(初步者)	beginner
C	n 초상화(肖像畵)	portrait
C	n 초순(初旬)	first ten days of a month
C	n 초여름(初-)	early summer
C	n 초원(草原)	plain
C	n 초저녁(初-)	early evening
C	n 초점(焦點)[-쩜]	focus

C	ⓐ 초조하다(焦燥-)	(be) irritated
C	ⓝ 초청(招請)(하)	invitation
B	ⓝ 초청장(招請狀)[-짱]	invitation (card)
C	ⓥ 초청하다(招請-)	invite
A	ⓝ 초콜릿[-릳]	chocolate
C	ⓐ 촌스럽다(村-)[-쓰-따]	(be) farmerly
C	ⓝ 촛불[초뿔]	candlelight
C	ⓡ 총(總)	total
C	ⓝ 총(銃)	gun
C	ⓝ 총각(總角)	unmarried man
C	ⓝ 총리(總理)[-니]	prime minister
B	ⓝ 총장(總長)	❶ secretary general ❷ president <university>
B	ⓝ 촬영(撮影)(하)[좌령]	photographing
B	ⓝ 최고(最高)	the best
C	ⓝ 최고급(最高級)	the highest grade
B	ⓝ 최근(最近)	most recent
B	ⓝ 최대(最大)	the greatest
C	ⓝ 최대한(最大限)	maximum
C	ⓝ 최상(最上)	the highest

B	n 최선(最善)	❶ the best
		❷ one's best
C	n 최소(最小)	the smallest
B	n 최소한(最小限)	minimum
C	n 최신(最新)	the newest
C	n 최악(最惡)	the worst
C	n 최저(最低)	the lowest
C	n 최종(最終)	the final
B	n 최초(最初)	the first
C	n 최후(最後)	❶ the end
		❷ one's death end
C	n 추가(追加)(하)	addition
C	v 추가되다(追加-)	be added
C	v 추가하다(追加-)	add
A	v 추다	dance
C	n 추석(秋夕)	Chuseok <holiday>
B	n 추억(追憶)(하)	remembrance
B	n 추위	cold weather
C	n 추진(推進)(하)	propulsion
C	v 추진하다(推進-)	promote

C	n 추천(推薦)(하)	recommendation
C	v 추천하다(推薦-)	recommend
C	n 추측(推測)(하)	guess
A	n 축구(蹴球)[-꾸]	soccer
B	n 축구공(蹴球-)[-꾸-]	soccer ball
C	n 축구장(蹴球場)[-꾸-]	football ground
C	n 축소(縮小)(하)[-쏘]	reduction
B	n 축제(祝祭)[-쩨]	festival
B	n 축하(祝賀)(하)[추카]	congratulation
A	v 축하하다(祝賀-)[추카-]	congratulate
B	n 출구(出口)	exit
C	n 출국(出國)(하)	departure from a country
B	n 출근(出勤)(하)	attendance (at office)
B	v 출근하다(出勤-)	go to the office
B	n 출발(出發)(하)	departure
C	n 출발점(出發點)[-쩜]	starting point
A	v 출발하다(出發-)	start
C	n 출산(出産)(하)[-싼]	childbirth
C	v 출석하다(出席-)[-써카-]	be present

C	n	출신(出身)[-씬]	native
C	n	출연(出演)(하)[추련]	①one's performance ②one's appearance (on the stage)
B	v	출연하다(出演-)[추련-]	①perform ②appear (on the stage)
B	n	출입(出入)(하)[추립]	①coming and going ②going out
C	n	출입국(出入國)[추립꾹]	entry into and departure from the country
B	n	출입문(出入門)[추림-]	entrance door
B	n	출장(出張)(하)[-짱]	business trip
C	n	출퇴근(出退勤)	commute
C	n	출판(出版)(하)	publishing
C	n	출판사(出版社)	publishing company
C	v	출현하다(出現-)	appear
A	n	춤	dance

A	ⓥ 춤추다	dance
A	ⓐ 춥다[-따]	(be) cold
B	ⓝ 충격(衝擊)	❶ shock ❷ hit
C	ⓝ 충격적(衝擊的)[-쩍]	shocking
C	ⓝ 충고(忠告)(하)	advice
C	ⓝ 충돌(衝突)(하)	❶ bump ❷ collision
C	ⓥ 충돌하다(衝突-)	❶ clash ❷ collide
B	ⓐ 충분하다(充分-)	(be) sufficient
B	ⓓ 충분히(充分-)	sufficiently
B	ⓝ 충청도(忠淸道)	Chungcheong-do <administrative>
A	ⓝ 취미(趣味)	hobby
B	ⓝ 취소(取消)(하)	cancellation
B	ⓥ 취소하다(取消-)	cancel
C	ⓝ 취업(就業)(하)	employment
C	ⓝ 취재(取材)(하)	subject selection
B	ⓝ 취직(就職)(하)	employment
B	ⓥ 취하다(取-)	❶ take ❷ choose
B	ⓥ 취하다(醉-)	❶ intoxicate ❷ get drunk

C	n 취향(趣向)	fondness
A	n 층(層)	floor
B	n 치과(齒科)[-꽈]	dental surgery
A	v 치다	beat (person), play (instrument), play (card)
C	v 치다	strike
C	v 치다	① count ② consider
C	v 치다	spread (a net)
B	n 치료(治療)(하)	medical treatment
C	n 치료법(治療法)[-뻡]	therapeutics
B	v 치료하다(治療-)	cure
C	v 치르다	① pay ② take
A	n 치마	skirt
C	n 치아(齒牙)	tooth
A	n 치약(齒藥)	toothpaste
B	v 치우다	① put in order ② eat off
C	s 치우다	final completion
B	n 치즈(cheese)	cheese

A ⓝ	친구(親舊)	friend
B ⓝ	친절(親切)(하)	kindness
A ⓐ	친절하다(親切-)	(be) kind
C ⓝ	친정(親庭)	parents' home of a married woman
B ⓝ	친척(親戚)	relative
B ⓐ	친하다(親-)	(be) intimate
C ⓥ	친해지다(親-)	become familiar
A ⓤ	칠(七)	seven
A ⓤ	칠십(七十)[-씹]	seventy
A ⓝ	칠월(七月)[치뤌]	July
A ⓝ	칠판(漆板)	blackboard
C ⓥ	칠하다(漆-)	❶ paint ❷ powder
C ⓝ	침	spittle
A ⓝ	침대(寢臺)	bed
C ⓝ	침묵(沈默)(하)	silence
B ⓝ	침실(寢室)	bedroom
C ⓐ	침착하다(沈着-)[-차카-]	(be) composed
A ⓝ	칫솔(齒-)[치쏠]	toothbrush
B ⓝ	칭찬(稱讚)(하)	praise
C ⓥ	칭찬하다(稱讚-)	praise

ㅋ

A ⓝ 카드(card)	card
B ⓝ 카레(curry)	curry
A ⓝ 카메라(camera)	❶ camera
	❷ movie camera
B ⓝ 카운터(counter)	(service) counter
B ⓝ 카페(프café)	cafe
C ⓝ 칸	space
A ⓝ 칼	knife
C ⓝ 칼국수[-쑤]	handmade knife-cut noodles
C ⓐ 캄캄하다	❶ (be) pitch-dark
	❷ (be) ill-informed
	❸ (be) gloomy
A ⓝ 캐나다(Canada)	Canada
C ⓝ 캐릭터(character)	character
B ⓝ 캠퍼스(campus)	campus
C ⓝ 캠페인(campaign)	campaign
B ⓐ 커다랗다[-라타]	❶ (be) big
	❷ (be) gigantic

B	ⓥ 커지다	grow large
B	ⓝ 커튼(curtain)	curtain
A	ⓝ 커피(coffee)	coffee
C	ⓝ 컨디션(condition)	condition (person, things)
C	ⓝ 컬러(color)	color
A	ⓝ 컴퓨터(computer)	computer
A	ⓝ 컵(cup)	cup
C	ⓝ 케첩(ketchup)	ketchup
A	ⓥ 켜다	turn on
B	ⓥ 켜지다	be turned on (light)
A	ⓝ 코	nose
C	ⓝ 코끝[-끋]	tip of one's nose
B	ⓝ 코끼리	elephant
B	ⓝ 코너(corner)	corner
C	ⓝ 코드(code)	code
C	ⓝ 코미디(comedy)	comedy
C	ⓝ 코스(course)	❶route ❷course ❸track
C	ⓝ 코스모스(cosmos)	cosmos<flower>

C	n 코치(coach)(하)	❶ training
		❷ coach
C	n 코트(court)	court (for sports game)
B	n 코피	nosebleed
B	n 콘서트(concert)	concert
A	n 콜라(cola)	cola
B	n 콤플렉스(complex)	complex <psychoanalysis>
B	n 콩	bean
B	n 콩나물	bean sprouts
C	n 쾌감(快感)	❶ happiness
		❷ pleasure
C	n 쿠데타(프coup d'État)	coup d'État
B	n 크기	size
A	v 크다	grow up
A	a 크다	(be) large
A	n 크리스마스(Christmas)	Christmas
C	n 크림(cream)	❶ cream
		❷ cosmetics
B	n 큰길	main road

C ⓝ 큰딸	one's eldest daughter
B ⓝ 큰소리(하)	loud voice
C ⓝ 큰아들[크나-]	one's eldest son
C ⓝ 큰아버지[크나-]	elder brother of one's father
C ⓝ 큰어머니[크너-]	wife of the elder brother of one's father
B ⓝ 큰일[-닐]	important matter
C ⓝ 큰절(하)	deep bow
C ⓝ 클래식(classic)	❶ classics ❷ classical
C ⓝ 클럽(club)	club (for the same purpose)
A ⓝ 키	stature
C ⓝ 키스(kiss)(하)	kiss
B ⓥ 키우다	bring up
B ⓝ 킬로(kilo)	kilo
B ⓝ 킬로그램(kilogram)	kilogram
B ⓝ 킬로미터(kilometer)	kilometer

ㅌ

C ⓥ 타고나다	be born with
A ⓥ 타다	❶ride ❷skate
C ⓥ 타다	mix
C ⓥ 타다	❶burn
	❷be anxious
	❸be sunburned
C ⓥ 타다	❶get (pays)
	❷get
C ⓝ 타락(墮落)(하)	depravity
C ⓥ 타오르다	❶blaze
	❷be anxious
C ⓝ 타입(type)	❶figure
	❷type
C ⓝ 타자기(打字機)	typewriter
C ⓓ 탁	❶unobstructedly
	❷suddenly
	❸spitting
C ⓝ 탁구(卓球)[-꾸]	table tennis
C ⓐ 탁월하다(卓越-)[타궐-]	(be) excellent

C	n 탁자(卓子)[-짜]	table
C	n 탄생(誕生)(하)	birth
C	v 탄생하다(誕生-)	be born
C	v 탈출하다(脫出-)	escape
B	n 탑(塔)	tower
C	n 탓(하)[탇]	reason
A	n 태권도(跆拳道)[-꿘-]	Taekwondo
B	n 태도(態度)	attitude
C	n 태아(胎兒)	unborn child
B	n 태양(太陽)	Sun
A	v 태어나다	be born
B	v 태우다	pick up (person)
B	v 태우다	set on fire
B	n 태풍(颱風)	typhoon
A	n 택시(taxi)	taxi
C	v 택하다(擇-)[태카-]	choose
B	n 탤런트(talent)	talent(of TV)
C	n 터	❶ foundation ❷ place
B	n 터	intention
B	n 터널(tunnel)	tunnel

B Ⓥ 터뜨리다	burst
B Ⓝ 터미널(terminal)	terminal (station)
C Ⓥ 터지다	❶ break
	❷ blow up
	❸ be disclosed
C Ⓝ 턱	reason
B Ⓝ 턱	chin
B Ⓝ 털	fur
B Ⓥ 털다	❶ shake off
	❷ be empty
C Ⓓ 텅	hollow
A Ⓝ 테니스(tennis)	tennis
C Ⓝ 테러(terror)	terror
B Ⓝ 테스트(test)(하)	❶ test ❷ exam
A Ⓝ 테이블(table)	table
B Ⓝ 테이프(tape)	❶ ribbon ❷ tape
C Ⓝ 텍스트(text)	text
A Ⓝ 텔레비전(television)	television
B Ⓝ 토끼	rabbit
C Ⓝ 토대(土臺)	❶ foundation
	❷ basis

B	ⓝ 토론(討論)(하)	discussion
C	ⓝ 토론자(討論者)	debater
C	ⓥ 토론하다(討論-)	discuss
C	ⓝ 토론회(討論會)	forum
B	ⓝ 토마토(tomato)	tomato
A	ⓝ 토요일(土曜日)	Saturday
C	ⓥ 토하다(吐-)	vomit
B	ⓝ 톤(ton)	ton
B	ⓝ 통(桶)	barrel
B	ⓝ 통(通)	copy
C	ⓝ 통계(統計)(하)[-게]	statistics
C	ⓝ 통과(通過)(하)	passing
C	ⓥ 통과하다(通過-)	pass
C	ⓝ 통로(通路)[-노]	passageway
B	ⓝ 통신(通信)(하)	communication
C	ⓝ 통역(通譯)(하)	interpretation
B	ⓝ 통일(統一)(하)	unity
C	ⓥ 통일하다(統一-)	unify
B	ⓝ 통장(通帳)	bankbook
C	ⓝ 통제(統制)(하)	control
C	ⓝ 통증(痛症)[-쯩]	ache

B	v	통하다(通-)	① pass
			② lead to
C	n	통합(統合)(하)	unification
C	n	통화(通貨)	currency
C	n	통화(通話)(하)	conversation by telephone
B	n	퇴근(退勤)(하)	leaving one's office
B	v	퇴근하다(退勤-)	leave the office
C	n	퇴원(退院)(하)	leaving hospital
C	v	퇴원하다(退院-)	leave hospital
C	n	퇴직금(退職金)[-끔]	retirement grants
C	a	투명하다(透明-)	(be) transparent
C	n	투자(投資)(하)	investment
C	n	투표(投票)(하)	voting
C	v	튀기다	spatter
C	n	튀김	fried-dish
C	v	튀다	① crack ② spatter ③ escape
C	v	튀어나오다	① shoot out ② rush out

C	n 트럭(truck)	truck
C	v 트이다	be opened
C	n 특급(特級)[-끕]	special grade
B	n 특별(特別)(하)[-뻘]	❶particular ❷excellence
B	a 특별하다(特別-)[-뻘-]	❶(be) special ❷(be) distinctive
B	d 특별히(特別-)[-뻘-]	specially
C	n 특성(特性)[-썽]	special quality
C	n 특수(特殊)(하)[-쑤]	speciality
C	n 특수성(特殊性)[-쑤썽]	particularity
C	a 특이하다(特異-)[트기-]	(be) peculiar
C	a 특정하다(特定-)[-쩡-]	(be) specific
B	n 특징(特徵)[-찡]	special feature
B	d 특히(特-)[트키]	especially
B	a 튼튼하다	❶(be) compact ❷(be) solid
C	d 튼튼히	strongly
C	n 틀	frame
B	v 틀다	turn
B	v 틀리다	❶be wrong

370

		❷ go bad
B	ⓐ 틀림없다[-리멉따]	(be) correct
C	ⓓ 틀림없이[-리멉씨]	certainly
C	ⓝ 틈	❶ crack ❷ leisure ❸ spare
A	ⓝ 티브이(TV)	TV
B	ⓝ 티셔츠(T-shirts)	T-shirts
A	ⓝ 팀(team)	team

ㅍ

B ⓝ 파	scallion
C ⓥ 파괴하다(破壞-)	destroy
C ⓥ 파다	dig
B ⓝ 파도(波濤)	wave
A ⓝ 파란색(-色)	blue color
B ⓐ 파랗다[-라타]	(be) blue
B ⓝ 파리	fly
B ⓝ 파리(Paris)	Paris
C ⓥ 파악하다[-아카-]	seize
B ⓝ 파일(file)	file
C ⓝ 파출소(派出所)[-쏘]	police box
A ⓝ 파티(party)(하)	party
C ⓝ 판	moment
C ⓝ 판	state of affairs
C ⓝ 판(板)	board
C ⓝ 판(版)	edition
C ⓝ 판결(判決)(하)	❶ decision
	❷ judgement
B ⓝ 판단(判斷)(하)	judgement

C Ⓥ	판단하다(判斷−)	judge
B Ⓝ	판매(販賣)(하)	selling
C Ⓥ	판매되다(販賣−)	be sold
B Ⓥ	판매하다(販賣−)	sell
C Ⓝ	판사(判事)	judge
A Ⓝ	팔	arm
A Ⓤ	팔(八)	eight
A Ⓥ	팔다	❶sell ❷divert
B Ⓥ	팔리다	be sold
A Ⓤ	팔십(八十)[−씹]	eighty
A Ⓝ	팔월(八月)[파뤌]	August
C Ⓝ	팝송(pop song)	pop song
B Ⓝ	패션(fashion)	fashion
B Ⓝ	팩(pack)	❶pack (for beauty) ❷pack (box)
C Ⓝ	팩스(fax)	fax
C Ⓝ	팩시밀리(facsimile)	facsimile
B Ⓝ	팬(fan)	fan
B Ⓝ	팬(pan)	pan
B Ⓝ	팬티(panties)	panties
A Ⓝ	퍼센트(percent)	percent

Korean Essential Vocabulary 6000 ❖ 373

C	ⓥ 퍼지다	❶ extend ❷ spread ❸ take air
C	ⓓ 퍽	very
C	ⓝ 페인트(paint)	paint (for the fence)
C	ⓥ 펴내다	publish
B	ⓥ 펴다	❶ unfold ❷ straighten ❸ unroll
C	ⓝ 편(便)	way
C	ⓝ 편	rather
B	ⓝ 편(篇)	book
C	ⓝ 편견(偏見)	prejudice
B	ⓐ 편리하다(便利-)[펼-]	(be) convenient
B	ⓐ 편안하다(便安-)[펴난-]	(be) peaceful
C	ⓝ 편의(便宜)[펴니]	convenience
C	ⓝ 편의점(便宜店)[펴니-]	convenience store
A	ⓝ 편지(便紙)	letter
B	ⓐ 편하다(便-)	❶(be) convenient

		❷ (be) comfortable
B	d 편히(便-)	peacefully
B	v 펼쳐지다	spread
C	n 평(坪)	❶ pyeong(unit of area)
		❷ a land measure of six square
C	n 평(評)	criticism
C	n 평가(評價)(하)[-까]	valuation
C	v 평가되다(評價-)[-까-]	be evaluated
C	v 평가하다(評價-)[-까-]	evaluate
C	n 평균(平均)(하)	average
B	a 평범하다(平凡-)	(be) common
C	n 평상시(平常時)	normal times
B	n 평생(平生)	lifetime
B	n 평소(平素)	ordinary times
C	n 평양(平壤)	Pyungyang
B	n 평일(平日)	weekday
B	n 평화(平和)	peace
C	a 평화롭다(平和-)[-따]	(be) peaceful
C	n 폐지(廢止)(하)[폐-]	abolition

C	ⓐ 포근하다	❶ (be) downy
		❷ (be) warm
B	ⓥ 포기하다(拋棄-)	give up
A	ⓝ 포도(葡萄)	grape
B	ⓝ 포도주(葡萄酒)	wine
B	ⓝ 포스터(poster)	poster (on the wall)
C	ⓝ 포인트(point)	❶ score
		❷ main point
B	ⓝ 포장(包裝)(하)	packing
C	ⓝ 포장마차(布帳馬車)	(wheeled) stall
C	ⓝ 포크(fork)	fork
C	ⓝ 포함(包含)(하)	inclusion
B	ⓥ 포함되다(包含-)	be included
B	ⓥ 포함하다(包含-)	include
B	ⓝ 폭(幅)	width
C	ⓐ 폭넓다(幅-)[퐁널따]	(be) broad
C	ⓝ 폭력(暴力)[퐁녁]	violence
A	ⓝ 표(票)	ticket
C	ⓝ 표(表)	tabular statement
C	ⓝ 표면(表面)	surface

C	n 표시(標示)(하)	mark
C	n 표시(表示)(하)	indication
C	v 표시하다(標示−)	indicate
B	v 표시하다(表示−)	express
B	n 표정(表情)	(facial) expression
C	n 표준(標準)	standard
B	n 표현(表現)(하)	expression
C	v 표현되다(表現−)	be expressed
B	v 표현하다(表現−)	express
C	v 푸다	pump
B	a 푸르다	(be) blue
B	d 푹	❶ with no gaps ❷ over(flap hat) ❸ thoroughly
B	n 풀	grass
B	n 풀	glue
B	v 풀다	❶ loose ❷ revenge(hatred)
B	v 풀리다	❶ abate ❷ thaw
C	v 풀어지다[푸러−]	get loose
C	n 품	❶ arm

C	ⓥ 품다[-따]	❷ magnanimity ❶ hold ❷ brood ❸ entertain
C	ⓝ 품목(品目)	item
C	ⓝ 품질(品質)	quality
B	ⓝ 풍경(風景)	landscape
C	ⓐ 풍부하다(豊富-)	(be) abundant
C	ⓝ 풍속(風俗)	customs
C	ⓝ 풍습(風習)	customs
A	ⓝ 프랑스(France)	France
B	ⓝ 프로	professional
B	ⓝ 프로	program(of TV)
B	ⓝ 프로그램(program)	program
C	ⓝ 프린터(printer)	printer
B	ⓝ 플라스틱(plastic)	plastic
B	ⓝ 피	blood
C	ⓝ 피곤(疲困)(하)	tiredness
A	ⓐ 피곤하다(疲困-)	(be) tired
B	ⓥ 피다	bloom
C	ⓝ 피디(PD)	PD(producer of TV)

B ⓝ피로(疲勞)(하)	fatigue
B ⓐ피로하다(疲勞-)	(be) fatigued
C ⓝ피망(프piment)	pimento
B ⓝ피부(皮膚)	skin
B ⓝ피시(PC)	personal computer
A ⓝ피아노(piano)	piano
A ⓥ피우다	smoke
A ⓝ피자(pizza)	pizza
C ⓥ피하다(避-)	avoid
C ⓝ피해(被害)(하)	damage
C ⓝ피해자(被害者)	victim
B ⓝ필름(film)	❶film ❷movie
C ⓝ필수(必須)[-쑤]	essentiality
C ⓝ필수적(必須的)[-쑤-]	essential
C ⓝ필연적(必然的)[피련-]	necessary
A ⓝ필요(必要)(하)[피료]	need
C ⓝ필요성(必要性)[피료썽]	necessity
A ⓐ필요하다(必要-)[피료-]	(be) necessary
C ⓝ필자(筆者)[-짜]	writer
B ⓝ필통(筆筒)	pencil case
C ⓝ핑계(하)[-게]	excuse

ㅎ

C ⓝ 하		below
C ⓓ 하긴		indeed
A ⓤ 하나		one
A ⓝ 하나		one
C ⓝ 하나님		God(Christian word)
C ⓓ 하나하나		one by one
C ⓝ 하나하나		one by one
C ⓝ 하느님		God, Heaven
A ⓝ 하늘		sky
A ⓥ 하다		do
A ⓢ 하다		❶ intend ❷ wish
C ⓓ 하도		too much
C ⓝ 하드웨어(hardware)		hardware
B ⓝ 하루		a day
C ⓝ 하룻밤[-루빰]		one night
C ⓝ 하반기(下半期)		second half of the year

B ⓝ	하숙집(下宿-)[-찝]	boardinghouse
C ⓝ	하순(下旬)	last ten days of a month
B ⓝ	하얀색(-色)	white color
B ⓐ	하얗다[-야타]	(be) very white
B ⓓ	하여튼(何如-)	anyhow
A ⓓ	하지만	but
C ⓝ	하천(河川)	river
B ⓝ	하품(하)	yawn
C ⓓ	하필(何必)	why necessarily
B ⓓ	하하	ha-ha
C ⓝ	학과(學科)[-꽈]	❶ department ❷ course
A ⓝ	학교(學校)[-교]	school
C ⓝ	학교생활(學校生活)[-교-]	school life
C ⓝ	학급(學級)[-끕]	class
B ⓝ	학기(學期)[-끼]	semester
A ⓝ	학년(學年)[항-]	scholastic year
C ⓝ	학력(學歷)[항녁]	academic background
C ⓝ	학번(學番)[-뻔]	student ID number

C ⓝ 학부모(學父母)[-뿌-]		parents of students
C ⓝ 학비(學費)[-삐]		school expenses
A ⓝ 학생(學生)[-쌩]		student
B ⓝ 학생증(學生證)[-쌩쯩]		student ID (card)
C ⓝ 학술(學術)[-쑬]		art and science
B ⓝ 학습(學習)(하)[-씁]		learning
C ⓝ 학용품(學用品)[하굥-]		school supplies
B ⓝ 학원(學院)[하권]		small private institute
C ⓝ 학위(學位)[하귀]		academic degree
C ⓝ 학자(學者)[-짜]		scholar
C ⓝ 학점(學點)[-쩜]		credit
A ⓡ 한		❶one ❷almost
C ⓝ 한(恨)		grudge
C ⓝ 한(限)		❶limit ❷as far as
C ⓝ 한가운데		very middle
C ⓐ 한가하다(閑暇-)		(be) free
A ⓝ 한강(漢江)		Han river
C ⓝ 한겨울		midwinter
C ⓓ 한결		remarkably

C n	한계(限界)[-게]	limit
C n	한구석	❶ corner
		❷ secluded place
A n	한국(韓國)	Korea
A n	한국말(韓國-)[-궁-]	Korean language
A n	한국어(韓國語)[-구거]	Korean language
B n	한국적(韓國的)[-쩍]	Korean
A n	한글	Korean alphabet
C n	한글날[-랄]	Hanguel Proclamation Day
B d	한꺼번에[-버네]	at a stretch
C n	한낮[-낟]	noon
C n	한눈	glance
C d	한데	one place, together
B n	한동안	for quite a time
B r	한두	one or two
B u	한둘	one or two
C n	한때	❶ same time
		❷ temperarily
B n	한라산(漢拏山)[할-]	Mt.Halla

C n	한마디	(single) word
C n	한문(漢文)	Chinese writing
C n	한반도(韓半島)	Korean Peninsula
C n	한밤중(-中)[-쭝]	midnight
A n	한번(-番)	for a time, once
A n	한복(韓服)	(traditional) Korean clothes
C n	한순간(-瞬間)	moment
B n	한숨	(deep) sigh
C n	한식(韓食)	Korean dishes
C n	한여름[-녀-]	midsummer
A n	한자(漢字)[-짜]	Chinese character
B n	한잔(-盞)(하)	drink (of liquor)
B v	한잔하다(-盞-)	have a drink
C v	한정되다(限定-)	be limited
C v	한정하다(限定-)	limit
B n	한쪽	one side
B n	한참	for some time
C d	한창	summit
C d	한층(-層)	still more
B d	한편(-便)	in the mean time

B n	한편(-便)	① one side ② on the other hand
C n	한평생(-平生)	all one's life
C v	한하다(限-)	restrict
A n	할머니	grandmother
A n	할아버지[하라-]	grandfather
B n	할인(割引)(하)[하린]	discount
A d	함께	together
C v	함께하다	share
B d	함부로	rudely
B n	합격(合格)(하)[-껵]	passing an examination
C v	합격하다[-껴카-]	pass an examination
C n	합리적(合理的)[함니-]	rational
B v	합치다(合-)	combine
C v	합하다(合-)[하파-]	combine
C n	항공(航空)(하)	flight
C n	항공기(航空機)	airplane
C n	항구(港口)	port

A	d 항상(恒常)	always
C	n 항의(抗議)(하)[-이]	protest
A	n 해	a year
A	n 해	Sun
C	n 해(害)(하)	harm
B	n 해결(解決)(하)	solution
C	v 해결되다(解決-)	be solved
B	v 해결하다(解決-)	solve
C	n 해군(海軍)	navy
C	v 해내다	accomplish
C	n 해답(解答)(하)	answer (to a question)
C	n 해당(該當)(하)	❶ correspond to ❷ resemble
C	v 해당되다(該當-)	be corresponded
C	v 해당하다(該當-)	correspond
C	a 해롭다(害-)[-따]	(be) harmful
B	d 해마다	annually
C	n 해물(海物)	seafoods
C	n 해석(解析)(하)	analysis
B	n 해석(解釋)(하)	interpretation

C	v 해석하다[-서카-]	interpret
C	n 해설(解說)(하)	explanation
C	n 해소(解消)(하)	settlement
C	v 해소하다(解消-)	be dissolved
C	n 해수욕장(海水浴場)[-짱]	swimming beach
C	n 해안(海岸)	coast
B	n 해외(海外)	overseas
B	n 해외여행(海外旅行)	overseas travel
C	n 핵(核)	nucleus
C	n 핵심(核心)[-씸]	❶ kernel
		❷ core
C	n 핸드백(handbag)	handbag
A	n 핸드폰(hand phone)	cell phone
C	n 햄(ham)	ham
A	n 햄버거(hamburger)	hamburger
B	n 햇볕[해뼡]	sunbeams
B	n 햇빛[해삗]	sunshine
B	n 햇살[해쌀]	sunlight
B	n 행동(行動)(하)	behavior
B	v 행동하다(行動-)	behave
B	n 행복(幸福)	happiness

B	ⓐ 행복하다[-보카-]	(be) happy
B	ⓝ 행사(行事)(하)	event
C	ⓝ 행사(行使)(하)	use
C	ⓝ 행운(幸運)	good luck
C	ⓝ 행위(行爲)	act
C	ⓥ 행하다(行-)	do
C	ⓥ 행해지다(行-)	be done
C	ⓝ 향(香)	incense
B	ⓝ 향기(香氣)	fragrance
C	ⓝ 향상(向上)(하)	improvement
C	ⓥ 향상되다(向上-)	be improved
B	ⓝ 향수(香水)	perfume
B	ⓥ 향하다(向-)	turn towards
C	ⓝ 허가(許可)(하)	permission
C	ⓝ 허락(許諾)(하)	approval
C	ⓥ 허락하다[-라카-]	admit
A	ⓝ 허리	waist
C	ⓝ 허용(許容)(하)	allowance
C	ⓥ 허용되다(許容-)	be permitted
B	ⓥ 허용하다(許容-)	permit
C	ⓓ 허허	ha-ha

B	r 헌	worn-out
C	v 헤매다	❶ hesitate ❷ struggle
C	v 헤아리다	❶ count ❷ fathom
B	v 헤어지다	❶ get scattered ❷ separate
C	n 헬기(helicopter機)	helicopter
B	n 혀	tongue
C	r 현(現)	present
B	n 현관(玄關)	porch
C	n 현관문(玄關門)	front door
B	n 현금(現金)	cash
B	n 현대(現代)	modern times
C	n 현대인(現代人)	moderners
C	n 현대적(現代的)	modern
C	n 현상(現象)	phenomenon
C	n 현실(現實)	reality
C	n 현실적(現實的)[-쩍]	realistic
C	n 현장(現場)	(actual) spot
B	n 현재(現在)	present (time)
B	d 현재(現在)	currently

B	n	현지(現地)	actual place
C	n	혈액(血液)[혀랙]	blood
C	n	협력(協力)(하)[혐녁]	cooperation
A	n	형(兄)	elder brother
C	n	형(型)	type
B	n	형님(兄-)	honorific of elder brother
B	n	형부(兄夫)	husband of a girl's elder sister
C	n	형사(刑事)	(police) detective
C	n	형성(形成)(하)	formation
C	v	형성되다(形成-)	be formed
C	v	형성하다(形成-)	form
C	n	형수(兄嫂)	wife of one's elder brother
C	n	형식(形式)	form
C	n	형식적(形式的)[-쩍]	formal
B	n	형제(兄弟)	brothers
C	n	형태(形態)	❶ shape ❷ form
C	n	형편(形便)	❶ situation ❷ family circum-

		stance
C	n 혜택(惠澤)[헤-]	benefaction
A	n 호(號)	number
C	n 호기심(好奇心)	curiosity
C	n 호남(湖南)	southwestern part of Korea
B	n 호랑이(虎狼-)	tiger
C	n 호박	pumpkin
B	n 호선(號線)	line number(of subway)
B	n 호수(湖水)	lake
C	n 호실(號室)	room NO.~
A	n 호주(濠洲)	Australia
C	n 호주머니(胡-)	pocket
A	n 호텔(hotel)	hotel
C	n 호흡(呼吸)(하)	breath
C	d 혹시(或是)[-씨]	rarely
B	d 혹은(或-)[호근]	or
C	v 혼나다(魂-)	❶ be horrified ❷ have an awful time

		❸ be scolded
A	ⓝ 혼자	alone
C	ⓝ 혼잣말[-잔-]	monolog
C	ⓓ 홀로	by oneself
B	ⓝ 홈페이지(homepage)	homepage
C	ⓝ 홍보(弘報)(하)	PR
C	ⓝ 홍수(洪水)	flood
B	ⓝ 홍차(紅茶)	red tea
A	ⓝ 화(火)	fire
B	ⓝ 화가(畫家)	painter
B	ⓥ 화나다(火-)	get angry
B	ⓐ 화려하다(華麗-)	(be) splendid
C	ⓝ 화면(畫面)	screen
B	ⓝ 화분(花盆)	flowerpot
C	ⓝ 화살	arrow
A	ⓝ 화요일(火曜日)	Tuesday
C	ⓝ 화장(化粧)(하)	cremation
A	ⓝ 화장실(化粧室)	rest room
C	ⓝ 화장지(化粧紙)	lavatory paper
B	ⓝ 화장품(化粧品)	cosmetics
C	ⓝ 화재(火災)	conflagration

C n	화제(話題)	topic of conversation
C n	화학(化學)	chemistry
C d	확	❶ with a jerk ❷ suddenly
B v	확대되다(擴大-)[-때-]	be enlarged
B v	확대하다(擴大-)[-때-]	enlarge
C v	확립하다(確立-)[황니파-]	establish
C n	확보(確保)(하)[-뽀]	guarantee
C v	확산되다(擴散-)[-싼-]	be diffused
C n	확신(確信)(하)[-씬]	conviction
C v	확신하다(確信-)[-씬-]	be convinced
B a	확실하다(確實-)[-씰-]	(be) certain
B d	확실히(確實-)[-씰-]	surely
B n	확인(確認)(하)[화긴]	confirmation
C v	확인되다[화긴-]	be confirmed
B v	확인하다[화긴-]	confirm
C n	확장(擴張)(하)[-짱]	expansion
C n	확정(確定)(하)[-쩡]	decision
B n	환갑(還甲)	one's 60th birthday anniversary

B	n	환경(環境)	environment
C	n	환경오염(環境汚染)	environmental pollution
B	n	환영(歡迎)(하)[화녕]	welcome
C	v	환영하다[화녕-]	welcome
C	n	환율(換率)[화뉼]	exchange rate
A	n	환자(患者)	patient
C	a	환하다	❶ (be) bright
			❷ (be) light-colored
			❸ (be) obvious
C	n	활기(活氣)	vigor
B	n	활동(活動)(하)[-똥]	activity
B	v	활동하다(活動-)[-똥-]	lead an active life
B	a	활발하다(活潑-)	(be) active
C	v	활발해지다(活潑-)	brisk
C	d	활발히(活潑-)	brisk
C	n	활용(活用)(하)[화룡]	practical use
B	v	활용하다(活用-)[화룡-]	utilize
C	d	활짝	❶ brightly <flower>
			❷ widely <door>

C	n	회(回)	round
C	n	회견(會見)(하)	interview
C	n	회관(會館)	assembly hall
C	n	회복(回復)(하)	recovery
C	v	회복되다(回復-)	recover
B	v	회복하다[-보카-]	recover
A	n	회사(會社)	company
B	n	회색(灰色)	gray color
B	n	회원(會員)	member
C	n	회의(懷疑)(하)[-이]	doubt
A	n	회의(會議)(하)[-이]	conference
B	n	회장(會長)	chairman (of a committee)
C	n	회전(回轉)(하)	❶ rotation ❷ turnover
B	n	회화(繪畵)	pictures
C	n	횟수(回數)[회쑤]	frequency
B	n	횡단보도(橫斷步道)	crosswalk
B	n	효과(效果)	effect
C	n	효과적(效果的)	effective
C	n	효도(孝道)(하)	filial duty

C	ⓥ 효도하다(孝道-)	be a good son
C	ⓝ 효율적(效率的)[-쩍]	efficient
C	ⓝ 효자(孝子)	faithful son
A	후(後)	❶ behind ❷ later
C	ⓝ 후기(後期)	latter term
C	ⓝ 후반(後半)	second half
B	ⓝ 후배(後輩)	❶ junior ❷ young generation
C	ⓝ 후보(候補)	candidate
B	ⓝ 후춧가루[-추까-]	ground pepper
C	ⓝ 후회(後悔)(하)	regret
B	ⓥ 후회하다(後悔-)	regret
C	ⓝ 훈련(訓鍊)(하)[훌-]	training
B	ⓐ 훌륭하다	(be) magnificent
C	ⓥ 훔치다	steal
B	ⓓ 훨씬	by far
B	ⓝ 휴가(休暇)	vacation
C	ⓝ 휴식(休息)(하)	rest
A	ⓝ 휴일(休日)	off day
A	ⓝ 휴지(休紙)	wastepaper

A	ⓝ 휴지통(休紙桶)	waste basket
C	ⓝ 흉내	mock
C	ⓥ 흐려지다	become dim
B	ⓥ 흐르다	flow
C	ⓝ 흐름	flowing
B	ⓐ 흐리다	(be) cloudy
C	ⓥ 흐리다	get muddy
C	ⓝ 흑백(黑白)[-빽]	black and white
C	ⓝ 흑인(黑人)[흐긴]	Black
B	ⓥ 흔들다	❶ shake ❷ wave ❸ upset
C	ⓥ 흔들리다	shake
C	ⓝ 흔적(痕跡)	traces
C	ⓐ 흔하다	(be) plentiful
B	ⓓ 흔히	frequently
B	ⓥ 흘러가다	flow
B	ⓥ 흘러나오다	flow out
C	ⓥ 흘러내리다	drop
B	ⓥ 흘리다	❶ spill ❷ shed ❸ pay no attention
B	ⓝ 흙[흑]	soil

B	ⓝ 흥미(興味)	interest
C	ⓐ 흥미롭다(興味-)[-따]	(be) interesting
C	ⓝ 흥분(興奮)(하)	excitement
C	ⓥ 흥분하다(興奮-)	be excited
C	ⓥ 흩어지다[흐터-]	scatter
C	ⓝ 희곡(戱曲)[히-]	drama
B	ⓐ 희다[히-]	❶(be) white ❷(be) snow-white
B	ⓝ 희망(希望)(하)[히-]	hope
C	ⓥ 희망하다(希望-)[히-]	hope
C	ⓝ 희생(犧牲)(하)[히-]	sacrifice
C	ⓥ 희생하다(犧牲-)[히-]	sacrifice
A	ⓝ 흰색(-色)[힌-]	white color
A	ⓝ 힘	power
C	ⓐ 힘겹다[-따]	(be) hard
C	ⓓ 힘껏[-껃]	as hard as one can
A	ⓐ 힘들다	(be) difficult
C	ⓥ 힘들어하다[-드러-]	be painful
C	ⓥ 힘쓰다	make an effort
C	ⓓ 힘없이[히멉씨]	dejectedly
C	ⓐ 힘차다	(be) energetic

Compiler **Lee Jae-wook**
   Ph.D. in Chinese Literature at Beijing University
   present <Beijing journal> editing member
   Beijing journal is one of newspapers for Koreans
   in China. He also serializes HSK jisanggangjwha,
   Geumjuchogeom on the newspaper.

Korean Essential Vocabulary 6000 For Foreigners

초판발행	2006년 7월 5일
초판 10쇄	2025년 2월 5일
저자	이재욱
편집	권이준, 김아영
펴낸이	엄태상
콘텐츠 제작	김선웅, 장형진
마케팅본부	이승욱, 왕성석, 노원준, 조성민, 이선민
경영기획	조성근, 최성훈, 김로은, 최수진, 오희연
물류	정종진, 윤덕현, 신승진, 구윤주
펴낸곳	한글파크
주소	서울시 종로구 자하문로 300 시사빌딩
주문 및 교재 문의	1588-1582
팩스	0502-989-9592
홈페이지	http://www.sisabooks.com
이메일	book_korean@sisadream.com
등록일자	2000년 8월 17일
등록번호	제300-2014-90호
ISBN	978-89-5518-489-1 13710

*한글파크는 랭기지플러스의 임프린트사이며, 한국어 전문 서적 출판 브랜드입니다.
*이 책의 내용을 사전 허가 없이 전재하거나 복제할 경우 법적인 제재를 받게 됨을 알려 드립니다.
*잘못된 책은 구입하신 서점에서 교환해 드립니다.
*정가는 표지에 표시되어 있습니다.